EUROPE UNDER STRESS

Butterworths European Studies is a series of monographs providing authoritative treatments of major issues in modern European political economy.

General Editor

François Duchêne   Director, Sussex European Research Centre, University of Sussex, England

Consultant Editors

David Allen   Department of European Studies, University of Loughborough, England

Hedley Bull   Montague Burton Professor of International Relations, University of Oxford, England

Wolfgang Hager   Visiting Professor, European University Institute, Florence, Italy

Stanley Hoffmann   Professor of Government and Director, Centre for European Studies, Harvard University, USA

Roger Morgan   Head of European Centre for Political Studies, Policy Studies Institute, London, England

Donald Puchala   Professor of Government and Director, Institute on Western Europe, Columbia University, USA

Susan Strange   Professor of International Relations, London School of Economics, England

William Wallace   Director of Studies, Royal Institute of International Affairs, London, England

Hanns Maull   Journalist, Bavarian Radio, Munich. Formerly European Secretary, Trilateral Commission, Paris

Already Published

Forthcoming Titles

Europe Under Stress

Convergence and Divergence in the European Community

Yao-su Hu

Published for

THE ROYAL INSTITUTE OF
INTERNATIONAL AFFAIRS

by

Butterworths

London Boston Sydney Wellington Durban Toronto

The Royal Institute of International Affairs is an unofficial body which promotes the scientific study of international questions and does not express opinions of its own. The opinions expressed in this publication are the responsibility of the author.

First published 1981

© The Royal Institute of International Affairs, 1981

British Library Cataloguing in Publication Data

Hu, Yao-su
  Europe under stress – (Butterworths European studies)
  1. European Economic Community – Economic policy
  I. Title
  330.94   HC241.2
  ISBN 0-408-10808-8

Photoset by Butterworths Litho Preparation Department
Reproduced from copy supplied
printed and bound in Great Britain
by Billing and Sons Limited and Kemp Hall Bindery
Guildford, London, Oxford, Worcester

Foreword

This is the second of two volumes which flow from a Chatham House project on the political implications of economic divergence in the European Community, funded by the Social Science Research Council. The first, *Economic Divergence in the European Community*, edited by Michael Hodges and William Wallace, was published in June 1981, bringing together a number of contributions by members of the research team and outside experts. This second volume offers an interpretation of the problems divergence poses for the European Community in a number of key sectors, from the perspective of a political economist.

Throughout the project the aim has been to combine, and compare, the political and economic aspects of European integration, and the distinctive approaches of economists and political scientists. Yao-su Hu came to the project as an economist with an established interest and expertise in European industrial policies, contributing to the arguments the point of view of the economist and rapidly redeploying this expertise to the political front. His scepticism about the processes of political integration partly reflects his inability to be persuaded that they were in any sense as predictable or as straightforward as those of economic integration.

Our aim in this project was also to avoid getting caught up too closely in immediate controversies, so as to examine the longer-term and underlying trends. This volume therefore examines a range of subjects in the fields of monetary, industrial, and trade policy which go well beyond the disputes of 1979–81 to gain, wherever possible, a wider view.

No new formulas have been offered for reversing divergent trends, for reinforcing political integration or resolving the dilemmas of economic integration. Instead, this book returns us to the realities of national interests and national powers, concepts which are very pertinent in illuminating the dynamics of Community developments.

William Wallace
Director of Studies, The Royal Institute of
International Affairs

Acknowledgements vii

Because this book has been particularly difficult to write, with a controversial subject-matter that cuts across the boundaries of economics and politics; extends over such fields as agriculture, monetary integration, the budget, trade and industry, and energy; involves arcane and esoteric details such as monetary compensatory amounts (MCAs) that change all the time; and addresses itself to an achievement, namely the European Community, about the nature and finality of which there is little consensus; the debt that I owe those who have helped and encouraged me is particularly great. While none of them is responsible for the remaining errors in this book, and while I doubt if any of them would agree with all the points that I make, I should like to take this opportunity to express my deep gratitude to them.

In Bonn a number of officials responsible for different aspects of German policy towards the European Community in different ministries gave me a great deal of help. I also benefited from discussions with several members of the British Embassy; I would particularly like to thank John Boyd, Economics Counsellor, for his assistance. Elsewhere in Germany, I benefited from exchanges of views at the Deutsches Institut für Wirtschaftsforschung, Berlin, the HWWA-Institut für Wirtschaftsforschung, Hamburg, and the Technische Universität Berlin.

In Brussels a large number of officials in the Commission provided advice and argument. I also learned much from conversations with members of the Council Secretariat, and of the British and German Representations to the European Communities. I would particularly like to thank Geoffrey Fitchew at the UK Representation for his help, as well as for his kindness in arranging interviews for me.

In Pairs, I would like to thank a number of members of the Commissariat Général du Plan, in particular of its Agriculture Section, and also members of the Institut National de Recherche Agronomique (INRA). My good friend Gérard Tardy, who has now moved from the Commissariat Général du Plan to Elf-Aquitaine, commented on an earlier draft of this book.

In London I have benefited much from the encouragement and comments of a number of officials in the Cabinet Office, the Foreign and Commonwealth Office, the Treasury, and the Department of Industry. Dr Georg Massion was very kind during his period as Minister at the German Embassy in London. Robert Jackson, member of the European Parliament, gave me incisive comments. Geoffrey Denton (Federal Trust and College of Europe) and John Pinder (Policy Studies Institute) have, as friends and mentors for many years, helped to sustain my morale in the face of this difficult book. Professor Susan Strange of the London School of Economics, Dr Roger Morgan of the Policy Studies Institute, and Wlodek Zajdlic, senior political economist at the Commercial Union, have given me detailed, lucid and encouraging comments. John Surrey and William Walker, both at the Science Policy Research Unit (SPRU), have helped me on energy questions, while Dan Jones at the Sussex European Research Centre and Keith Pavitt at SPRU have reminded me of the perennial problem of the lack of industrial dynamism in the United Kingdom. William Wallace has been both a Director of Studies and a friend. Jean Pell, who worked part of her time for me as secretary, has been a tower of strength in difficult moments. I would also like to thank the staff of the two Chatham House libraries for their expert assistance and patience.

Finally, I must thank my wife and children, who have had to endure the nervous tension and physical absence that this project has entailed, and my parents, who have had both to put me up and to put up with me during the finalization of the text.

London, February 1981   *Yao-su Hu*

The Royal Institute of International Affairs and its Research Committee are grateful for the comments and suggestions made by John Pinder and Professor Susan Strange, who were asked to review the manuscript of this book.

List of Abbreviations

CAP	Common Agricultural Policy
CCP	Common Commercial Policy
EAEC	European Atomic Energy Community (= Euratom)
EAGGF	European Agricultural Guidance and Guarantee Fund
EC	European Community
ECs	European Communities, i.e. ECSC, EEC and EAEC
ECSC	European Coal and Steel Community
ECU	European Currency Unit (= EUA)
EEC	European Economic Community
EIB	European Investment Bank
EMCF	European Monetary Co-operation Fund
EMF	European Monetary Fund
EMS	European Monetary System
EMU	Economic and Monetary Union
ERDF	European Regional Development Fund
EUA	European Unit of Account (= ECU)
Euratom	*See* EAEC
FEOGA	*See* EAGGF
GATT	General Agreement on Tariffs and Trade
IEA	International Energy Agency
IMF	International Monetary Fund
MCA	Monetary Compensatory Amount
MFA	Multi-Fibre Agreement
OECD	Organization for Economic Co-operation and Development
OPEC	Organization of Petroleum Exporting Countries
PPP	Purchasing-Power Parity
VAT	Value Added Tax

Contents

Introduction

The post Second World War period of high growth and low inflation, which appears in retrospect as a golden age of Western capitalism, came to an end with the 1973–4 oil crisis, if not earlier (already by 1968 a rise in inflation rates and the beginning of international currency upheavals could be detected). During the 1970s, low growth and high inflation, which at first were thought to be temporary phenomena, persisted year after year, with no end in sight in the 1980s to the general economic crisis in the West. The economic crisis affected different countries unevenly, or one could say that it brought out into the open and further accentuated the differences between the different economies. This phenomenon of divergent or uneven developments and performances between countries could be observed both for the OECD as a whole (including the USA and Japan) and at regional level in the EEC. Not only did inflation in general rise (from 5 per cent per annum or less on average during the greater part of the 1950s and 1960s, to 10 per cent or more on average since 1974, for the OECD area as a whole), but the magnitude of the differences in inflation rates between the low-inflation and the high-inflation countries increased dramatically (with, for example, an inflation rate of more than 20 per cent in some years in the United Kingdom and Italy and a rate that has been contained to below 6 per cent in most years in the Federal Republic of Germany). The low-inflation countries have had a tendency for their currencies to appreciate on the foreign exchange markets, while the high-inflation countries have seen more or less continuous depreciation of their currencies (except for the pound sterling during the last year or two, due largely to the impact of North Sea oil). This combination gave rise to the distinction between strong and weak economies. In terms of growth and unemployment, the differences have been less marked than in terms of inflation and exchange rates, but the strong economies appear to have (so far) weathered the storm better than the weak economies, and differences in per capita incomes have persisted or increased further. The strong economies may also be more successful in redeploying or adjusting the structure of their output and trade, thus laying the basis for a further consolidation and accentuation of the gap that separates them from the weak economies.

Since the first oil crisis of 1973–4, 'convergence' and 'divergence' have become two of the most frequently used words in statements of European

Community policy. Convergence figures prominently as a leading, if not the leading, goal of most Community policies, and has apparently replaced 'integration' or 'the construction of Europe' in terms of popularity. Take, for example, some recent meetings of the European Council, i.e. the European summit of the Heads of State and Government of the member states. The Resolution of the European Council meeting in Brussels in December 1978 stated, among other things:

> 'We stress that, within the context of a broadly-based strategy aimed at improving the prospects of economic development and based on symmetrical rights and obligations of all participants, the most important concern should be to enhance the *convergence* of economic policies towards greater stability. We request the Council [Economics and Finance Ministers] to strengthen its procedures for co-ordination in order to improve that *convergence*.
>
> 'We are aware that the *convergence* of economic policies and of economic performance will not be easy to achieve. ... The European Council requests the Commission to study the relationship between greater *convergence* in economic performance of the member states and the utilization of Community instruments, in particular the funds which aim at reducing structural imbalance. ...' [Italics added.]

And, according to the Conclusions of the Presidency at the Paris meeting of the European Council in March 1979:

> 'The European Council ... had an exchange of view on the means for arriving at improved *convergence*. ... It invited the Council and the Commission to examine in depth how the Community could make a greater contribution, by means of all its policies taken as a whole, to achieving greater *convergence* of the economies of the Member States and to reducing the disparities between them. ... [Italics added.]

Divergence, on the other hand, has been described as an ominous development that could undermine the very existence of the Community. Thus, Anthony Crosland, in his presidential speech before the European Parliament on 12 January 1977, remarked that divergences in national economic performance had increased 'to an extent that in practice rules out major measures of integration'. David Owen, in his first major speech as Foreign Secretary, went further in asserting that 'there could be little doubt that, were the present trends of economic divergence to become firmly established, they would present a serious threat to the cohesion of the Community'[1]. Thus, the concepts of convergence and divergence appear to go to the heart of the European Community's development and survival.

The purpose of this book is twofold. The direct goal is to examine and clarify the concepts of convergence and divergence, and to attempt to assess the political implications of economic convergence/divergence for the

Community, that is to say, for both Community policies and for its member states. The wider purpose of this book is, it is hoped, to contribute to a better understanding of the nature of the European Community and of the forces that shape its development, i.e. of its dynamics, through the concepts of convergence/divergence and the approach that has been adopted in this book as a result of these concepts. These points are explained and developed in the rest of this chapter.

Definition and concept

In defining convergence/divergence, we must avoid two pitfalls. It is important to avoid too narrow a definition that would severely limit our use of the terms within the context of current usage at the European and national levels. It is also necessary to avoid such a loose definition as to permit an almost indiscriminate use of the terms.

According to dictionaries, to diverge (*diverger* in French, *auseinan-dergehen* in German) means, of two or more elements, to move away or to proceed in different directions from a point or from each other, in other words to move further and further apart. To converge means to move towards each other or a common point. Divergence and convergence are therefore *dynamic* notions; they indicate certain types of movements over time, whereas words such as 'difference', 'disparity', and 'similarity' denote *static* concepts and refer to a comparison at a fixed point in time.

To take a restricted definition, divergence can be defined as a process whereby certain differences or disparities increase in intensity over time, or come into existence where they did not exist before; convergence can be defined as a process whereby initial differences or disparities decrease in intensity over time, or whereby an increasing degree of similarity comes about. In such a restricted definition, divergence and convergence refer to how the degree of disparity or similarity changes over time.

My own experience in adopting such a definition has led me to the conclusion that it has a paralysing effect and creates a gap with current usage in policy statements and other utterances. At the same time, I believe that it is important not to use divergence to characterize any difference, or convergence to characterize any similarity. There would then be no end to the list of phenomena that would come under divergence or convergence. Any difference could be seized upon as constituting divergence in the EEC and a threat to its cohesion, and we would be led to the absurd view that the survival of the EEC requires the levelling out of each and every difference between member states.

I therefore propose that divergence/convergence be used simply to indicate difference/similarity in a *dynamic* sense, without too much prior concern for what it is that constitutes the dynamic element. Thus, for example, differences in economic performance may be considered to be dynamic and hence to constitute economic divergence, in the following senses (by no means exhaustive): (a) the differences did not exist or were negligible in a previous period; (b) the differences persist over time; (c) the differences increase in intensity over time; (d) the differences are subject to cumulative causation, with vicious or virtuous circles operating; (e) the differences have dynamic consequences or tend to pull the countries apart; (f) the differences are between *rates* of increase rather than *levels*.

Such a definition may appear unsatisfactory from a scientific point of view. However, as Sir Karl Popper said[2]:

'The precision of a language depends, rather, just upon the fact that it takes care not to burden its terms with the task of being precise. ... In science, all the terms that are really needed must be undefined terms.'

Moreover, I believe that the definition proposed above accords best with current usage.

Apparent confusion: policy, performance or what?

In theory, economic divergence/convergence can refer to the divergence/convergence of economic performances or to the divergence/convergence of economic policies. In practice, however, it is useful to bear in mind that, whereas economic divergence is an observable phenomenon or set of phenomena over the last decade or more, convergence is mostly used as a normative concept to denote a proposed goal or objective for the European Community.

As an empirical phenomenon, divergent economic developments result both from the policies adopted and from the performance of the economies concerned. In this sense, the distinction between divergence of economic policies and divergence of economic performance is rather meaningless. Moreover, the same indicators, e.g. exchange rate movements, may point either to economic performance (an appreciating exchange rate may reflect a good performance in controlling inflation) or to economic policy (the government may decide to allow the exchange rate to depreciate in order to help exports).

As a normative concept, as a proposed goal, convergence is open to different interpretations and emphases. Mr Roy Jenkins, President of the Commission of the European Communities, said in a speech to the European Parliament on 14 November 1979:

'Convergence may be an obfuscating rather than a clarifying word, because it can mean different things to different people. To some it means little more than the better co-ordination of economic policies. To others it is a code word for dealing with the problem of the budget, while to others still it means the transfer of resources to produce more consistent standards of living within the Community.'

There is nothing surprising in this. In international politics and diplomacy, it is natural and normal for the protagonists to give different meanings to the same word, especially when that word has political appeal and represents an irresistible rallying cry. In order to understand the different meanings of such a term, the student of international politics cannot limit himself to a linguistic analysis. He should examine the different arguments advanced by the parties involved which revolve around such a word, and relate such arguments to the interests, concerns and perceptions of the various parties. In international politics, words are used and arguments advanced, not for their scientific value *per se*, but for political purposes and to further certain perceived interests. In order to understand certain key words and arguments, the student of international politics should ask: by whom is a particular interpretation and argument advanced, and what are the interests that could be served by adopting such a position?

The confusion about the meaning of convergence is only apparent; it should not deceive the politically sensitive *cognoscente*. Convergence has a very definite meaning for the less prosperous member states of the EEC, which call for 'the convergence of economic performance or achievements', and a different but equally precise meaning for the Federal Republic of Germany, whose position is expressed in terms of 'the convergence of economic policies'. The different meanings of convergence and their implications are analysed in the subsequent chapters.

When convergence refers to the *convergence* of policies, its meaning becomes very close to that of *co-ordination* or *co-operation*. It may, however, be interesting to speculate on the differences or nuances. As it has evolved during the 1970s, the international co-ordination of economic policies, both within the EEC and at 'world economic summits' (Rambouillet in 1975, Puerto Rico in 1976, London in 1977, Bonn in 1978, Tokyo in 1979, and Venice in 1980), has in practice meant little more than the exchange of views and of information resulting in the issuance of common declarations of intent at a very general level. In contradistinction to this, convergence means *rapprochement*, which implies that the different national policies are actually brought closer together. Co-ordination, on the other hand, may mean working towards a common objective, and need not entail any actual *rapprochement* of different national policies.

Convergence and divergence of perceived national interests

The dichotomy in official statements between convergence of economic policies and convergence of economic performance leaves out, in my view, a major dimension of the problem, namely, the divergence and convergence of perceived national *interests*. This silence is perhaps due to prudishness and the desire to be seen as 'good Europeans', but it has created a yawning gap between Community rhetoric and reality.

> 'The idea of interest is indeed the essence of politics. ... Thucydides' statement, born of the experiences of ancient Greece, that "identity of interests is the surest of bonds whether between states or individuals" was taken up in the nineteenth century by Lord Salisbury's remark that "the only bond of union that endures" among nations is "the absence of all clashing interests". It was erected into a general principle of government by George Washington: "A small knowledge of human nature will convince us that, with far the greatest part of mankind, interest is the governing principle."'[3]

Despite the rhetoric, European affairs are no exception to this general rule. According to one who was at many European negotations[4]:

> 'More present even than Europe is the national reality of each. Can one avow "without shame" that the function of the negotiator is to make the interests of his country prevail and not to carry through European negotiation? The attitude is not only avowable, it is in evidence.'

Although national interests are rooted in 'objective' factors such as geography and history, the same objective factors can give rise to different interpretations of the national interest and to the adoption of different options in foreign policy. What matters in international politics, therefore, is not some independently given national interests, but national interests as perceived and interpreted by those who have the power and the responsibility of defending them in the international arena, i.e. primarily national governments. Governments are subject to many pressures; in defining the national interest for foreign policy purposes, they have to arbitrate between the claims of the various groups in the country, make trade-offs between the short and the long term, choose between the desirable and the attainable, and deal with imponderables. In all this, perceptions play a crucial role. Changes in perceived national interests come about as a result of changes in governments, changes in national attitudes, changes in the internal balance of political power, etc.

The convergence and divergence of perceived national interests will be a major theme of this book. It may be objected strongly that the European Communities are a unique historical experience attempting to transcend national interests, that Community language is a major instrument to help achieve this, and that therefore to raise explicitly the question of national interests is a bad thing. This is a very serious charge, especially in view of the high hopes and enthusiasm that had been raised by the European movement. The answer depends on whether one believes that language and rhetoric can influence human nature and change reality, or whether one believes that it is less harmful to face reality and to avoid contortions that can easily degenerate into hypocrisy and lead to even worse results than in their absence. To quote the founder of the modern school of political realism again[3]:

> '... if we look at all nations, our own included, as political entities pursuing their respective interests ... we are able to do justice to all of them. And we are able to do justice to all of them in a dual sense: we are able to judge other nations as we judge our own and, having judged them in this fashion, we are then capable of pursuing policies that respect the interests of other nations, while protecting and promoting those of our own. Moderation in policy cannot fail to reflect moderation of moral judgement.'

Moreover, what matters is *perceived* national interests. Common interests are not only those which are naturally so, but also those which are made and perceived to be common. The hope for Europe is that, as member states gain the habit of working together, their perceptions of their own national interests will increasingly shift from a short-term nationalistic outlook to a long-term European perspective. But this is a process that takes time, particularly in view of the difference of history, language and culture.

Divergence between whom?

Regional disparities within the EEC are an important issue, but, from the point of view of the *political* significance of economic divergence for the Community, what matters is the divergence between member states. The difficulties and disagreement that affect the Community are between the member states, not directly between the regions. Certainly, the regions enter into the calculations of national interests, and the regional policy arguments are used in Community institutions to further certain member states' claims on the Community budget. The regions, however, are not autonomous actors on the scene; their demands are expressed through the governments of the nations of which they are parts; there are no direct dealings between the European Community and the regions, certain member states having made sure that the disbursement of Community regional aid is via the national governments and only for regional projects which are presented to the Community by the national governments; and there is thus no genuine common regional policy (the European Regional Development Fund — ERDF — is still very small, amounting to 5 per cent of the Community's budget or less).

Divergences between the regions of the EEC should therefore be seen in the context of divergences between the member states.

The approach adopted in this book

The aims of this book and the concepts of divergence and convergence have dictated an approach which can be characterized under three headings.

Firstly, the approach cuts across the boundaries of the economics and political science disciplines. Too often, the political scientists fail to follow up apparently technical issues that nevertheless may have important political implications, while the economists refrain from thinking through the political consequences of economic developments, and their proposals suffer from insufficient account being taken of their political feasibility.

Secondly, as against general and abstract works, the technical literature has tended to look at policies and problems in isolation, one at a time, without trying to show the connections and common themes between them or giving much thought to the overall meaning of the multifarious developments in different sectors. The symposium technique does not remedy this deficiency, because the different chapters are often written by different authors. The reader is still left wondering 'what it's all about'. Besides general reflections on the European Community, this book will look at a number of policy areas (agriculture, the budget and resource transfers, energy, trade and industry, the EMS) which have been selected because of their actual or potential importance to the Community's development. Given the number of policy areas involved and the complexity of each, the intention is not to examine each sector exhaustively nor is it to provide an in-depth technical analysis, but to highlight certain critical issues in order to give substance to the general themes. This admittedly quixotic attempt has been dictated by the political nature of the decision-making process in the Community, in which progress on one issue often depends on progress on other issues and difficulties on one front can lead to paralysis on others, inasmuch as national governments do not bargain or negotiate on just one issue in isolation, but across issues, in what has been called the 'package-deal' approach.

Thirdly, this book sees the European Community, European Communities, or EEC as made up of sovereign member states but also as a system with certain historically unique supranational features. The Community is not a political union in which the member states are akin to the provinces or counties within a unitary state or to the states or Länder in a federal state; the unanimity rule for decision-making in the Council and the fact that the European Court of Justice does not dispose of independent powers of enforcement against the member states' governments are clear indications of this. As against this, the Community should not be compared simply to a bargaining forum such as the United Nations or the multilateral trade negotiations under the General Agreement on Tariffs and Trade (GATT[5]). There is a higher degree of political commitment, as most member states have invested, over the years, a great deal of hope and political capital in the construction of the European edifice, and the decisions reached by the Community are legally binding, while regulations have direct legal applicability in all member states.

Because of the complex nature of the Community, it does not appear very useful to look at it purely from the point of view of what happens in the supranational institutions in Brussels, Luxembourg or Strasbourg; one should also look at what happens in the member states. At the same time, one should also avoid seeing the Community simply from the point of view of one single country, one's own. Cost–benefit calculations of EEC membership for one country, for example, are very different from attempts to understand the dynamics of the Community's evolution. Thus this book is about the Community as a framework in which sovereign nation states interact with each other and with the supranational features of the system.

The chapters in Part One examine the attitudes of the major EEC member states to the convergence/divergence issue and what the terms mean for each of them, and attempts to relate these positions to the concerns and interests of the countries concerned. The chapters in Part Two attempt to analyse the impact of economic divergence on Community policies.

1 *Hansard*, 1 March 1977.
2 Karl Popper, *The Open Society and Its Enemies*, London, Routledge, 1945.
3 Hans J. Morgenthau, *Politics Among Nations*, 5th edn., New York, 1978.
4 Edgard Pisani, 'Pratique de la négotiation européenne', *Pouvoirs*, No. 15, Winter 1980. (My translation – Y.S. H.)
5 As some American political scientists, who have turned away from the concept of integration to that of interdependence, tend to do. See, for example, Donald J. Puchala and Hugh V. Balaam, 'National autonomy and the European Communities', paper presented to the European-American Seminar held in Tilburg (the Netherlands) in June 1979. Puchala and Balaam argued (p. 9): 'Though its sectoral jurisdiction is broader; its secretariat more complex, independent, aggressive, and perhaps imaginative; and its institutions more elaborate, the EC, in its internal functioning, actually looks a great deal like

the GATT. That is to say, an international economic regulatory agency that manages interdependence among industrial states by setting rules of preferred conduct which are adhered to because of member states' self-interest and acceptance.'

For the literature on interdependence, see, for example, Robert O. Keohane and Joseph S. Nye, *Power and Interdependence*, Boston, Mass., Little, Brown, 1977; Richard N. Cooper, *The Economics of Interdependence*, New York, N.Y., McGraw-Hill, 1968; and the collection of essays in: OECD, *From Marshall Plan to Global Interdependence*, Paris, 1978. The theory of interdependence, if it can be called a theory, often appears to be lacking in precision and in specific predictions, in comparison with the earlier literature on European integration (e.g. Ernst Haas, *The Uniting of Europe*, Stanford, Calif., Stanford University Press, 1958).

Member states

In analysing the impact and significance of economic divergence and convergence, the European Community can be looked at in at least two ways: in terms of the interrelationships between the member states and the Community, and in terms of the major areas of Community policy. The next three chapters take the first point of view.

In human affairs as well as in political analysis, it is useful to bear in mind that there are two orders of reality which are closely intertwined. On the one hand, there are raw facts and events, which can be described in chronologies and statistical tables. On the other, there are the perceptions and interpretations of this raw material by the protagonists involved. Such perceptions constitute facts no less than chronologies and statistics, and are often more important in terms of policy consequences.

There has been some excellent work on economic divergence as a statistical phenomenon[1]. Without the intervention of perceptions of national interests, however, statistical indicators are, by themselves, incapable of revealing the nature and significance of the problem as a political problem.

In what follows, the emphasis is on the second of the two orders of reality, with statistical tables being adduced to illustrate the points being made rather than for their own sake. How do the major member states view the convergence/divergence issue? What do they mean when they call for the Community to promote economic convergence? How are the differences of meanings related to the countries' situations, concerns, perceptions and interests? What is at issue in the debate, and what are the implications for the future of the European Community? These are the questions that are addressed.

---

1 Both the November 1978 and the November 1979 issues of *European Economy* (published by the Commission of the European Communitites) contain a chapter on Convergence and Divergence. See also the statistical annex by E. C. Hallett in M. Hodges and W. Wallace (eds.), *Economic Divergence in the European Community*, London, Allen & Unwin, 1981.

Economic Stability and the Convergence of Economic Policies

For the Federal Republic of Germany, convergence means essentially the adoption by its EEC partners of economic policies designed to bring down their rates of inflation and to align them on the lower German level. This position appears to have been motivated by five factors: (a) a strong interest in maintaining free trade throughout the European Common Market; (b) a historically rooted fear of, some would say a neurosis about, inflation, and the belief that inflation could easily undermine the Common Market; (c) the increase in inflation rates and in the magnitude of their dispersion in the 1970s; (d) a strong desire bordering on the obsessive for economic and political stability; (e) a natural reluctance to commit German financial resources to the assistance of partner countries unless the Federal Republic has a say in the way they run their economies.

Divergence of inflation rates

Looking back, the fifties and sixties appear as a golden age for Western capitalism, combining prosperity with price stability. There is, however, a great deal of controversy as to when and why this golden period came to an end. Taking inflation first, the underlying rate of inflation[1] has more than doubled in the major Western industrial countries, from 5 per cent per annum or less, on average, during the greater part of 1950s and 1960s, to 10 per cent per annum or more on average since the crisis began in 1974.

Taking the nine present member states of the European Community as a whole, the average rate of inflation never rose above 4 per cent in each year between 1959 and 1968 (*Table 2.1*), while the weighted standard deviation remained below 2 in each of those years (except in 1959, when France was bringing inflation under control under General de Gaulle and the Rueff Plan). On average for the ten years, the Federal Republic of Germany had a lower rate of inflation than the others, but the difference was very small: 2.4 per cent per annum compared to 3.8 per cent for France, 3.4 per cent for Italy, 3.0 per cent for the United Kingdom, and 3.1 per cent for the Nine.

This happy state of affairs began to change, almost imperceptibly at first, even before the oil-price shocks of 1973–4. The change may well have started in France first, where the rate of inflation in 1969 went over the 6 per

Table 2.1 EEC countries: annual rates of change in consumer prices 1959–78 (per cent)

Year	Belgium	Denmark	France	Federal Republic of Germany	Ireland	Italy	Netherlands	United Kingdom	EEC total[1]	Weighted standard deviation[2]
1959	1.2	1.8	5.7	1.0	0.0	0.5	0.9	0.6	1.8	2.220
1960	0.3	1.2	4.1	1.2	0.4	2.4	2.5	1.0	2.1	1.290
1961	0.9	3.5	2.4	2.5	2.8	2.1	1.6	3.4	2.5	0.604
1962	1.5	7.3	5.2	3.0	4.3	4.6	1.9	4.3	3.9	1.267
1963	2.1	6.2	5.2	2.9	2.5	7.5	3.8	1.9	4.0	1.833
1964	4.2	3.1	3.1	2.4	6.7	5.9	5.5	3.3	3.5	1.224
1965	4.1	6.5	2.5	3.4	5.0	4.6	4.0	4.8	3.7	0.959
1966	4.2	6.7	2.7	3.5	3.0	2.3	5.8	3.9	3.5	0.996
1967	2.9	6.9	2.7	1.4	3.2	3.2	3.5	2.5	2.5	1.022
1968	2.7	8.6	4.5	2.6	4.7	1.4	3.7	4.7	3.5	1.428
1969	3.8	4.2	6.4	1.9	7.4	2.6	7.4	5.5	4.2	2.035
1970	3.9	5.8	5.2	3.4	8.2	5.0	3.7	6.4	4.8	1.153
1971	4.3	5.8	5.5	5.3	8.9	4.8	7.5	9.4	6.1	1.634
1972	5.5	6.6	5.9	5.5	8.7	5.7	7.8	7.1	6.1	0.746
1973	7.0	9.3	7.3	6.9	11.4	10.8	8.0	9.2	8.1	1.381
1974	12.7	15.3	13.7	7.0	17.0	19.1	9.6	16.0	12.7	4.299
1975	12.8	9.6	11.7	6.0	20.9	17.0	10.2	24.2	12.9	6.335
1976	9.4	9.0	9.6	4.5	18.0	16.8	8.8	16.5	10.3	4.779
1977	7.1	11.1	9.8	3.9	13.6	17.0	6.4	15.9	9.9	4.959
1978	9.4	9.9	9.1	2.4	7.6	12.1	4.1	8.3	6.6	3.456
1979	4.5	9.8	10.7	5.0	13.3	14.8	4.2	13.4	10.0	4.094
1980[3]	7.6	10.7	13.5	5.3	18.2	22.0	6.7	15.3	11.8	5.525

1 Including Luxembourg, which is not shown separately.
2 The weights used are relative gross domestic products (GDP).
3 Annualized rate based on the first eleven months of the year.
Source: OECD, Main Economic Indicators, various issues up to January 1981.

cent mark for the first time for eleven years, and may have spread to Germany last (perhaps in 1970), but the average rate of inflation for the Nine went over the 4 per cent mark in both 1969 and 1970, and over the 6 per cent mark in the two following years. In 1973, on the eve of the oil crisis, it was already standing at 8.1 per cent. The timing of this acceleration of inflation leads one to treat with some scepticism the assertions of those who attribute all the economic ills of the West to the petroleum-producing nations.

In statistical terms, the divergent evolution and sizeable dispersion of inflation rates in Europe was brought about by two factors – the dramatic rise in inflation throughout the West and its uneven or unequal impact on individual countries, particularly as between the 'strong' and the 'weak' economies, as they have come subsequently to be designated. Inflation rose in all countries, but it increased much more in some than others. In the United Kingdom, the rate of inflation shot up to 16 per cent per annum in 1974 to reach a peak of 24 per cent in 1975, and the government was eventually forced to borrow from the International Monetary Fund (IMF) and to impose stabilization measures. The rate of inflation was brought down to near 8 per cent in 1978, but rose to more than 15 per cent (annualized) in 1980. In Italy, the rate of inflation rose to a peak of 19 per cent in 1974, and, despite a gradual decrease to about 12 per cent in 1978, increased to 22 per cent in 1980. In France, the peak of nearly 14 per cent was reached in 1974, and the rate of inflation was brought under 10 per cent in 1976, 1977 and 1978, but since then increased consecutively in 1979 and 1980. Of all the major EEC countries, only Germany succeeded in containing inflation – to 7 per cent in 1974 and to below 6 per cent since then.

The Benelux countries, however, have tried to follow the German example, a task which was facilitated to some extent by their close trade links and cultural affinity with Germany and by their joining the currency snake centred on the Deutschmark. Although inflation reached peak levels of near 13 per cent in Belgium and around 10 per cent in the Netherlands in the two years 1974–5, it was brought down to below 5 per cent in the Netherlands in 1978 and 1979, and in Belgium in 1979, before rising again in 1980. In interpreting the acceleration in inflation rates in 1980, the second oil shock, following the Iranian revolution, is a major factor to be borne in mind.

The weighted standard deviation of the Nine's inflation rates, which (with the exception of 1969) had been below the value of 2 in the 1960s, rose to 4.3 in 1974 and 6.3 the following year. Since then, there has been limited convergence in the sense of reductions in inflation differentials, but the disparities still remain much larger than before 1974, with 1980 rates ranging from 5.3 per cent in Germany to 22 per cent in Italy. It appears that the divergent evolutions of inflation rates have left differences in these rates which may persist for a long time.

The standard deviation is an indicator that measures dispersion around the average. Measured in relation to the lowest level, namely the German level, the degree of disparity would appear considerably greater than that suggested by the standard deviation, since the average has been pulled up by the poor performance of Germany's partner countries, in particular the United Kingdom and Italy.

Why should these developments worry the Federal Republic?

Inflation and the Common Market

The Germans are concerned about rising inflation because, in the words of a high official, 'unless inflation is brought under control, the principle of the Common Market is in danger in every respect'. Inflation is a very dangerous sickness that feeds upon itself, and can easily get out of control. When this happens in a particular country, the latter inevitably comes under increasing pressure to tamper with the principle of free trade. As exports become uncompetitive and imports are sucked in (because of their increasing price advantage and/or excess demand in the domestic economy), the trade balance and employment are adversely affected, and, if the exchange rate does not fall fast enough, the demands for protectionist measures (and perhaps also export subsidies) become increasingly difficult to resist. If, conversely, the fall in the exchange rate accelerates, the rise in import prices fuels the forces of inflation, a vicious and accelerating circle (of higher inflation, lower exchange rate, still higher inflation, and so on) may set in, and massive capital flights may then take place. The currency may then become unacceptable on the foreign exchange markets, the country's international creditworthiness may collapse, and the government may then be forced to impose restrictions not only on trade but also on international payments and foreign exchange transactions. In any event (the Germans reason), it is not too difficult to invent new barriers to trade and payments.

In 1976, for example, after inflation had been running for two years at annual rates of 19 and 17 per cent in Italy, the government imposed a special deposit scheme to penalize importers, and then added a 10 per cent import surcharge, at the same time as it was seeking loans from the IMF, the EEC and the Federal Republic of Germany. In the same year, after inflation had reached, in 1975, an unprecedented annual rate of 24 per cent in the United Kingdom the pound fell to below US$ 1.6 at one stage, and the government could no longer rely on the swap agreement between the Bank of England and the other central banks of the Group of Ten as its creditworthiness had apparently been exhausted; it had to turn to the international lender of the last resort, the IMF, and to resist strong demands for protectionism emanating from within the Labour Party. In German eyes, the survival of the Common Market came close to being seriously threatened by the near collapse of two major member states in 1976.

The Federal Republic of Germany is, of course, not alone in having a strong interest in the maintenance of free trade in the EEC. The Benelux countries and France are more dependent on the EEC market than Germany: in 1978, for example, 72 per cent of the Benelux's total exports and 53 per cent of France's total exports went to the EEC, compared with 46 per cent for the Federal Republic. The German position is, however, noteworthy for a number of reasons. The first is that the Federal Republic is the major economic power in the EEC and that, to have a chance of success, any EEC policy initiative must have German financial support. German views therefore carry particular weight. Secondly, German economic success has been particularly dependent on exports, and the Federal Republic is the biggest exporting nation in the world. In 1979, for example, it accounted for 20.7 per cent of total OECD exports of manufactures, compared with 13.6 per cent for Japan, 15.9 for the USA, 10.5 for France, and less than 10 per cent for the United Kingdom and Italy respectively. The Federal Republic is therefore strongly interested in the maintenance of free trade world-wide, but within the global system, the EEC is of particular interest to it. The EEC represents not only the largest export market for Germany (representing 46 per cent of its total exports in 1978, compared with 34 per cent ten years ago), but also, qualitatively, the most secure and open market; for the EEC has attained, within itself, a much higher degree of trade liberalization than in the rest of the OECD or the world, a liberalization which, moreover, is based on legal commitments and political agreements that are much more binding and solid than those underpinning the GATT system.

German interest in the EEC is also political. For historical and geo-strategic reasons, German diplomacy still appears inhibited in comparison with that of France or the United Kingdom, despite the country's economic weight. Membership of the European Community increases its options and enhances its influence internationally.

It follows that the preservation of the existence and cohesion of the European Community as a free-trade area (internally) and as a system of political co-operation must rank high among German priorities. The Germans, however, have an extraordinary fear of inflation, because of the indelible impressions left on the collective memory by the great inflation of the 1920s, and this reinforces their almost desperate search for stability. In German thinking, inflation is a most deadly menace to political and economic stability, both at home and abroad. Economic divergence in the sense of divergent inflation rates in the EEC is seen not only as a problem, but also as a very serious danger.

The danger is that of partner countries going over the brink of economic, financial and political collapse through allowing inflation to get out of hand.

These countries would then need to be assisted, and because of Germany's economic weight, it would have to fund a major share of the bill, whether directly or through the IMF or the EEC. The countries in difficulty might impose trade and payment restrictions, thus undermining the Common Market and hurting German exports. Worse still, they might go communist or fascist, thus undermining Western political stability and the international *ordnung*.

Calls for the convergence of economic policies

Hence the Federal Republic has been leading the calls in the EEC for the 'convergence of economic policies'. This expression may need a little explanation. In the German view, control of inflation is essentially a matter of self-discipline, of the political will and courage to adopt 'sound policies'. The Germans apparently tend to play down the importance of those historically conditioned attitudes and structures that make for consensus in Germany and social and political strife in some other countries. Thus the convergence of economic policies stands for the convergence of inflation rates. Moreover, the different inflation rates should converge, not towards the average (as this would mean that Germany should raise its rate of inflation towards the Community average and would therefore be totally unacceptable to it), but towards the 'lowest possible level' [22], in other words, the German level.

As for the convergence of per capita income levels, the German view sometimes appears to be that this is not a major issue for the European Community. Even in the USA, with its much higher degree of economic integration and political unification than the European Community, there are still sizeable income differentials. This problem is taken up in Chapter 9.

The concern about inflation is not new in the EEC. As early as 1956, the Spaak report[3] said:

'... divergence in monetary evolution or in the rhythm of activity of different countries may transform the price relationships or the rhythm of trade so suddenly that a common market is not conceivable without common rules, common actions and finally an institutional system to watch over them.' (p. 14)

. . . .

'... the divergences in the level of economic activity or in that of prices ... are the principal causes of balance-of-payments disequilibria. ... Such divergences could modify suddenly the conditions of competition in a common market. Every effort must be made to avoid them or to overcome the effects.' (p. 17)

After more than a decade of relative price stability and calm on the international monetary scene, convergence came back on to the stage with the EEC sumit meeting at The Hague in December 1969. The Heads of State and Govenment called for the creation, in stages, of an Economic and Monetary Union (EMU). Article 8 of the final communique stated;

> 'The development of monetary co-operation should be backed up by the harmonization of economic policies.
>
> 'They [the Heads of State and Government] agreed to arrange for the investigation of the possibility of setting up a European Reserve Fund as one ultimate result of pursuing a common economic and monetary policy.'

This position was taken up in the Werner report[4] which declared, in its conclusions: '... in particular, the development of monetary unification must be articulated on parallel progress in the area of the convergence and then the unification of economic policies.'

In the debate over the implementation of EMU which opposed them, the 'monetarists' led by France argued for monetary integration first, while the 'economists' led by the Federal Republic of Germany emphasized the need to make economic policies converge first. One interpretation of the 'economists'' position was that Germany had sensed that it would have to finance a major share of the costs of monetary union, and was reluctant to do so unless it could have some say in the way its partners ran their economies. There was no question of Germany underwriting what it considered to be the profligacy of certain governments.

EMU came to little. Then came the European Monetary System (EMS). The question of convergence was given an importance of the first order. Witness the resolution about the creation of the EMS which was adopted by the European Council (of Heads of State and Government) in Brussels in December 1978, which states[5]:

> 'We stress that, within the context of a broadly-based strategy aimed at improving the prospects of economic development ... the most important concern should be to enhance the convergence of economic policies towards *greater stability*' [italics added].

The insistence on the convergence of economic policies *within* the context of the EMS establishes a linkage between access to the financial assistance available under the scheme (the financing and credit mechanisms for market intervention and balance-of-payments purposes, and the interest rebate scheme on Community loans to the less prosperous member states) and full subscription to the discipline which the EMS entails and the convergence of economic policies towards greater stability. In return for German underwriting of a major share of the financial assistance available, it establishes German *mitspracherecht* over the other participants' economic policies.

The debate

It has been argued that the convergence of economic policies (in the German sense) may not result in a convergence of economic performance, because of 'structural' differences between countries. Thus, in a weaker economy, the same restrictive policy may only succeed in reducing employment and growth to a greater extent, while pulling inflation down to a much smaller degree, than in Germany. Or, to achieve the same level of price stability as in Germany, the deflationary pressure and hence unemployment would have to be much greater. The German argument is that inflation, far from being a stimulant, is bad for growth and employment, and that controlling inflation is above all a matter of self-discipline and political will. In the last three or four years, there has been an apparent convergence of economic philosophy and policy towards the German model, with restrictive monetarist-oriented policies being adopted in Italy, France (under the premiership of M. Raymond Barre) and the United Kingdom (first under the former Labour chancellor, Mr Denis Healey, and now with intensified rigour under the Conservative Government of Mrs Thatcher). Yet inflation rates in these three major EC economies have not been brought down to anywhere near the German level and, after decelerating for a while, are on the increase again since 1979, despite the high rate of unemployment. Meanwhile, unemployment has continued to increase, particularly in the United Kingdom, stimulated no doubt by the deflationary policies. At this point, the debate is likely to turn towards questions such as whether unemployment is structural (i.e. cannot be absorbed by increasing aggregate demand), whether growth is held back by lack of demand or by lack of profitable investment opportunities, whether real wages are too high for full employment, and whether the West can absorb the shock of the latest oil price rises.

These questions are hard – if not impossible – to settle intellectually. It may, however, be pointed out that, for historical reasons, Germany enjoys a degree of social consensus and trade-union self-restraint that is difficult to replicate in the other three major EC member states, which have a much more active element of class struggle and/or trade-union problems; and that it is probably much easier to absorb and attenuate social conflicts through controlled and moderate redistribution (without at the same time provoking excessive inflation) when the economy is strong and living standards already high in comparison with what people can remember. Nonetheless, it is undeniable that two-digit inflation rates can easily get out of control and have highly destabilizing effects in economic, political and social terms.

Summary and conclusions

The Federal Republic of Germany emphasizes the convergence of economic policies, which means the adoption by its partners in the EEC of policies designed to align their inflation rates on the German level. The Germans have a strong interest in the maintenance of free trade and stability in the European Community, and they see inflation as a prime danger to both. The call for convergence in the context of the EMS establishes a link between German underwriting of the financial assistance available under the EMS and an undertaking by other participants to promote the convergence of economic policies 'towards greater stability'. Two unresolved questions remain: to what extent actual convergence of policies will produce convergence of results and to what extent the Germans will be willing to underwrite the EMS by providing large amounts of financial assistance and by exposing themselves (as they see it) to the risk of imported inflation.

1 As measured by the consumer price index.

2 This is certainly the view of the Bundesbank, which enjoys much power in the Federal Republic. See the article on the EMS in the *Monthly Report of the Deutsche Bundesbank*, March 1979; and: Otmar Emminger, 'The exchange rate as an instrument of policy', *Lloyds Bank Review*, July 1979.

3 Comité intergouvernemental créé par la Conférence de Messine. *Rapport des chefs de délégations aux ministres des affaires étrangères*, Brussels, April 1956. (My translations – Y.S.H.)

4 This was the report by the committee set up to work out the plan for EMU in stages, in pursuance of the decision made at The Hague; see the *Rapport au Conseil et à la Commission concernant la réalisation par étapes de l'union economique et monétaire dans la Communauté*, Luxembourg, October 1970.

5 This was the first paragraph of Section B, which was entitled 'Measures Designed to Strengthen the Economies of the Less Prosperous Member States of the EMS', of the Resolution on the EMS. Section A was entitled 'The European Monetary System' and concerned its mechanisms.

Power, National Interests, and Franco-German Convergence

At the Community level, the debate about convergence and divergence is about the weaker economies in relation to the stronger ones. In France, however, the discussion has a distinct flavour, and is conducted more in national than in Community terms. For France, the essence of the convergence/divergence problem, indeed the *leitmotif* of the construction of Europe, has been posed in terms of the age-old problem of relations with Germany. Convergence means above all the *rapprochement with Germany in both world and European affairs, and catching up with Germany in terms of economic power.*

The German problem and the construction of Europe

From about the middle of the nineteenth century to the middle of the twentieth, the history of Europe had been dominated by the German problem. This problem has had two components: the natural superiority of Germany on the continent in terms of industrial and military power, and the reluctance of the other countries, especially France, to accept this German superiority and a Europe under German hegemony. France tried to solve the problem by building up a system of alliances and coalitions in an endeavour to maintain a balance of power. This, however, did not prevent the outbreak of two murderous world wars, in which the 'sons of France' were butchered, and what saved France in the two wars was the intervention of Great Britain and the USA.

The construction of a united Europe represented a new solution to this age-old problem. It is noteworthy that the initiatives for such a Europe, at least in the early 1950s, came from France. France had the active support of the Benelux countries, which remembered only too clearly that the Franco-German wars had been fought over their territories, and of Germany, which, utterly disgraced by the Hitler aberration, was striving to reconstitute a nation, to obtain international respectability and to regain admission to the concert of nations.

Basically, the new solution consisted in drawing Germany firmly into Europe's arms so as to render German power innocuous to its neighbours, to disarm Germany rather than oppose it. Following the method proposed by Jean Monnet European peace and unity were to be achieved through concrete solidarities. The first achievement was the European Coal and Steel Community, established by the Treaty of Paris signed in 1951. Coal and steel were extremely logical candidates with which to begin the construction of a united Europe, since they were widely perceived to constitute the basis of industrial and military power. A pooling of the French and German industries under supranational management would therefore make further wars with Germany materially impossible, it was thought. The same considerations underlay the French initiative in calling for a European Defence Community. If, as the Americans were insisting in view of the Cold War, the Germans were to rearm, better that they should rearm under European control than under their own or American control. In the event, this was too much for French nationalism, and the venture was vetoed by the French National Assembly in 1954. By the time the Treaty of Rome establishing the European Economic Community was signed, in 1957, economic considerations had gained the ascendancy over politico-military matters.

Political and diplomatic convergence or *rapprochement*

General de Gaulle, master of political realism, was fully cognizant of the German problem, of the importance of Franco-German relations in determining the future of Europe, and of the limits of the supranational route towards a united Europe (for which nation would voluntarily relinquish its sovereignty?). Unlike Ludwig Erhard and the economists, who emphasized free trade and the global system, for Chancellor Konrad Adenauer the *raison d'être* of Europe was above all political. Based initially on a Gaullist vision of an intergovernmental Europe under Franco-German leadership, the Franco-German Friendship Treaty was signed in January 1963, but the statements which the Bundestag insisted on including as an addendum vitiated General de Gaulle's efforts from the start. In the decade that followed, the treaty came to little. There were a number of reasons for this, including the personal relations between de Gaulle and Adenauer's successor, Ludwig Erhard, conflicts over the establishment of the Common Agricultural Policy (CAP) which led to the 'empty chair' crisis in 1965 (whereby France boycotted Community institutions), and conflicts over the United Kingdom's application to join the EEC. One of the principal reasons, however, was the incompatibility for Germany of both unconditionally following US leadership in world, European and NATO affairs and seeking closer co-operation with France, at a time when France and the United States were often in a state of open dispute.

By the time that Valéry Giscard d'Estaing and Helmut Schmidt became leaders in their respective countries in 1974, many of the issues that divided their two countries had been resolved. The CAP had become an *acquis communautaire*: its definitive financing, for which the French had fought very hard, had been enshrined in the Community's decision to establish its Own Resources, in return for which President Pompidou had agreed to British membership of the Community. Under President Giscard d'Estaing, France had been adopting a less abrasive and more conciliatory attitude towards the United States, while at the same time the Federal Republic of Germany was beginning to move further and further away from unconditional support for the United States, with whom it has had major disputes during the 1970s, e.g. over the dollar's instability, the US failure to curb its energy imports, and German exports of nuclear reactors. The personal friendship between the two European leaders, German disillusionment with the role of the United Kingdom in the EC since its membership[1], and uncertainties about the world situation, about the credibility of the US commitment to defend Europe, and about the quality of US leadership, have given further impetus to Franco-German relations, which have become closer and closer[2], to the point where the French President could declare, in February 1977 during one of his regular meetings with his German counterpart, that 'the Franco-German entente constitutes the cornerstone of all progress in the construction of Europe'[3], and where other countries have come to fear or envy the Franco-German 'directorate'. Such is the centrality of the two countries in Europe and their combined weight (in 1979 the two countries accounted for 56 per cent of Community gross domestic product at market exchange rates) and the demonstrated ability of the two governments to work together at the levels of heads of state or government, ministers and senior civil servants, that, on matters ranging from the launching of the EMS to the speed of the second round of enlargements (to include the Mediterranean countries), it is no great exaggeration to say that what the European Community agrees to do is what the two agree to do. Often the outcome of meetings of the European Council can be gauged in advance by observing the bilateral meetings between the two leaders in Paris or Bonn.

Thus, for the French, one of the principal connotations of convergence is simply the new-found *rapprochement* in European and world affairs between France and Germany, succeeding more than a century of enmity and war. To what extent is this convergence dependent on the holding of office by the present leaders? Only the future can tell, but an important consideration is that the two countries have learnt to work together and, in the process, have created a number of common interests. For common interests are not only those which are naturally so, but also those which are made and perceived to be common. Thus, Franco-German convergence is based on a convergence of perceived interests.

Convergence of economic power

If the Franco-German alliance is to remain an equal partnership and not degenerate into German domination, France must maintain a certain balance in the two countries' overall power relationships. For those who are opposed to the alliance for nationalistic reasons (the Gaullists and the French Communist Party), the need to maintain French power in relation to the Federal Republic goes without saying. A balance in the overall *rapport de forces* means, in the economic sphere, that France has to strive to catch up with Germany, or at any rate, that it cannot allow its economic power to fall too far behind that of Germany. When the French compare their economic performance with that of the Federal Republic and other countries, economic power is a major criterion; this is shown by the way they look at gross domestic product (GDP), the importance attached to population figures, and the emphasis on industry and industrial competitiveness.

Table 3.1 *Increase in the volume of GDP (per cent per annum)*

	1960–70	1971	1972	1973	1974	1975	1976	1977	1978	1979
Belgium	4.9	4.1	5.7	6.4	4.7	−2.2	5.6	1.2	2.5	3.0
Denmark	4.9	2.4	5.4	5.2	0.6	−1.2	6.3	1.9	0.9	1.8
France	5.6	5.4	5.9	5.4	3.2	0.2	5.0	2.8	3.3	2.9
Germany	4.7	3.2	3.7	4.9	0.5	−1.8	5.2	2.7	3.2	4.3
Ireland	4.2	4.1	5.7	4.6	2.1	1.2	2.9	5.6	6.1	2.8
Italy	5.6	1.6	3.1	6.9	4.2	−3.5	5.9	2.0	2.6	4.3
Luxembourg	3.6	4.1	5.9	10.2	4.7	−9.4	2.9	1.7	3.2	2.5
Netherlands	5.4	4.4	3.9	5.9	4.2	−1.0	5.3	2.8	2.4	2.6
United Kingdom	2.8	2.6	2.3	7.9	−1.8	−1.7	3.6	1.2	3.7	0.3
EC	4.6	3.4	4.0	6.0	1.6	−1.6	5.0	2.3	3.1	3.1
Japan	10.7	7.3	8.9	9.8	−1.0	2.4	6.0	5.4	5.6	5.7
USA	3.8	2.9	5.8	5.4	−1.3	−1.0	3.5	4.9	4.0	1.5
OECD	4.8	4.0	5.5	6.3	0.5	−1.0	5.1	3.9	3.8	2.9

Source: EC Commission, *European Economy*, November 1979.

During the 1960s France enjoyed, together with Italy, the highest growth rate among the Nine (*Table 3.1*). Between 1960 and 1970, French GDP grew at an average rate of 5.6 per cent per annum, outstripping Germany's 4.7 per cent by almost one whole percentage point. This French lead in growth, which continued until 1975, gave rise to hopes of catching up with Germany, and was a favourite theme of official French thinking. It found expression, for example, in the largely government-inspired Hudson Institute report[4] in 1973, which opened with the statement:

> 'France today possesses the most dynamic economy in Europe ... France can hope to be, in ten years, the most powerful European economy in terms of total production.'

There is, however, a difference between relative GDP growth and relative GDP levels in absolute terms. Statistically, GDP growth is measured in volume terms and does not take direct account of the effect of changes in the exchange rate. When compared at actual or market exchange rates, GDP levels can go up or down because of changes in the country's exchange rate. Compared with 1958 and with 1968, the gap between French and German total GDP levels widened subsequently (*Table 3.2*), to a large extent because of the devaluation of the franc in 1958, and the downward and upward floating of the franc and Deutschmark respectively since 1969 (from an approximately equal par value the mark rose in value to reach around 2.3 French francs in the summer and autumn of 1980). Whereas France was close to catching up with the Federal Republic in 1958 and 1968, by 1979 the gap was 100 to 75. In other words, there has been *divergence*.

Table 3.2 *Relative GDP, at current prices and exchange rates*

Year	Federal Republic of Germany	France	United Kingdom	Italy
1958	100	99	109	51
1963	100	86	89	52
1968	100	93	77	56
1973	100	73	51	41
1979	100	75	51	43

Source: EC Commission, *European Economy*, November 1979 and March 1980.

Table 3.2 also gives an idea of the extent of the United Kingdom's relative decline, such that France has now become the only country standing between a Community dominated by German economic power a more balanced Europe.

It is revealing that the French tend to focus more on total GDP rather than only GDP per capita and to make the comparisons at market or actual exchange rates (rather than at purchasing-power parities – PPPs)[5]. GDP per capita indicates income levels or living standards, while total GDP is an indication of a country's total production or economic weight. The use of market exchange rates points to a country's ability to sustain international transactions (trade, investment abroad, aid, repayment of debt, etc.); 'it translates the country's international purchasing power'[6]. This is because international transactions are conducted in actual currencies, which are converted into each other at market exchange rates. Relative standards of living, on the other hand, depend on domestic purchasing power, which is what PPPs attempt to reflect (see Chapter 4). It is true that the continuous revaluation of the Deutschmark since the end of the 1960s 'distorts' the comparison at market exchange rates, to the disadvantage of France, but a strong currency may be seen *precisely* as a sign or even an essential ingredient of a country's international economic power and status. 'The FRG compensates over the period for a slower growth in volume by a stronger valorization [of the mark] in international money.'[6]

Another indication that it is relative economic power or weight that concerns France is the importance attached to French population growth in relation to other countries. Economic power is a question not only of income levels but also of total GDP. As long as an increase in population does not depress income levels (i.e. as long as the eventual marginal contribution of population to GDP is positive and exceeds the average income level) it may be considered to contribute to the nation's economic power. In addition, the size of population may contribute to the nation's military potential and international cultural influence. Clemenceau has been quoted as saying, during the First World War, that there were twenty million Germans too many. Since the Second World War, the *nataliste* policies pursued by successive French governments have been among the most active and generous in the world, ranging from generous family and children's allowances to maternity leave and benefits, and reductions for travel on the French railways for large families. Cries of alarm can often be heard from ministers and politicians about the dangers of a slow-down in population growth. This is in marked contrast to the attitudes in many other European countries, which tend to emphasize economic welfare or well-being rather than economic power and consider that it is easier to provide for a smaller population, and which in any case do not seem to worry too much about population growth being low or negative.

There is also a great interest in international comparisons of the evolution of industrial structures, whereby the competitiveness of French industry is assessed and countries are ranked in first, second and third divisions in the international league[7]. There is a much more explicit recognition of the importance of industry and industrial exports than in, say, the United Kingdom; industry is considered to be the basis of a country's economic and military power, and economic growth is seen to be largely determined by industrial growth and international competitiveness. Changes in the structure of output and of exports and imports (i.e. their breakdown into major branches or products) are eagerly scrutinzed on a comparative basis as providing advance indicators of changes in competitiveness; in other words, the focus is on *structural divergence and convergence*.

A good example is contained in the Maldague report[8]. Industrial products are divided into three broad categories: those incorporating low-skilled labour and facing intense competition from the new industrial countries of the Third World; products with a high skilled-labour intensity; and products 'fundamental for the control of the international division of labour' which are subdivided into the technological control, intermediate goods and principal capital goods categories. The major OECD countries are then ranked according to the evolution over 1963, 1970 and 1977 of three indicators: an export specialization index, an index of relative dependence on imports, and a market-share index. As with many similar studies, the Federal Republic of Germany, Japan and the USA are found to be in the first division, the United Kingdom and Italy in the bottom list, and France in an intermediate position. Unfortunately, the implications of this kind of analysis for Community policies (as distinct from national policies) are seldom clearly spelt out, and the classification of industrial products by categories may not be as precise as it seems. Nevertheless, this kind of product-by-product and industry-by-industry approach is a great step forward in comparison with the undifferentiated macro-economic approach, which tends to be obsessed with aggregate demand or the money supply.

Convergence of economic philosophies and policies

Since the slow-down in the growth of the French economy after the 1973–4 oil crisis, French fascination with the German model has been enhanced[9] under President Giscard d'Estaing and his Prime Minister, M. Raymond Barre. The policies of M. Barre with their apparent emphases on the control of inflation, the liberalization of controls, and the redeployment of industry are presented as a direct attempt to model French economic policy on Germany. French sponsorship of the EMS has been partly motivated by a belief that by maintaining or enhancing the external value of the franc industry would be forced to improve its efficiency, productivity and structural composition, while import costs and inflation would be restrained at home, a vision of a 'virtuous circle' that is based on a certain interpretation of the German experience in the 1970s. This strategy is, however, open to question in that, by squeezing profit margins in export industries, it may reduce industrial investment and hence the productivity growth and industrial redeployment that it ostensibly seeks to achieve[10]. Meanwhile, political discourses abound in references to the 'German model', with the traditional Gaullists and the Communists accusing the government of selling out to German diktat or US–German hegemony. In this context, convergence refers to the real or alleged alignment of French economic policies on the German model. Thus Franco–German *rapprochement* or convergence in the foreign policy field has apparently been extended into French domestic economic policy.

It may be noted, however, that, with the emergence of a current-account deficit in Germany in 1980 and with the apparent recent weakening of German industry's competitive edge in relation to that of Japan, French interest may be shifting from the German model to the Japanese model[11]. The latter is more in line with French traditions of central direction and close industry–government relations than the German rhetoric of the market economy and government non-intervention[12], and the concept of key industries is shared by the French and the Japanese.

Summary and conclusions

For France, the problem of convergence is defined primarily in terms of the Federal Republic of Germany. The *rapprochement* between the two countries has been based on a convengence of perceived interests; their ability to work together and their combined weight in the European Community have given the Franco-German alliance *de facto* leadership of the Community. The French are also concerned to catch up economically with Germany, or at least not to allow their economic power to fall too far behind that of the Federal Republic, and economic power is a major criterion in French assessments of convergence/divergence. The French are also interested in studies of structural convergence/divergence, but the implications for Community policies (as distinct from national policies) are by no means clear. Finally, there has been under President Giscard d'Estaing and Prime Minister Raymond Barre an apparent convergence of economic philosophy and policies towards the German model. Whether this will lead to a convergence of results remains to be seen, but French interest seems to be shifting to the Japanese model.

1 This was clearly brought out in several of Schmidt's open declarations. See, for example, an interview published by *The Economist*, 29 September 1979, in which he said: 'I have hoped for a greater role of Britain within the EEC than has emerged so far. ... I have not so far really been satisfied by England's role in Europe.'

2 On the Franco-German alliance, see: James O. Goldborough, 'The Franco-German entente', *Foreign Affairs*, April 1976; David Lawday, 'The odd couple', *The Economist*, 26 May 1979; Jonathan Story, 'The Franco-German alliance', *The World Today*, June 1980.

3 *Le Monde*, 5 February 1977.

4 Hudson Institute, *L'envol de la France*, Paris, 1973.

5 See, for example, a book by the staff of *Le Monde*, *Vingt ans de réussite allemande*, Paris, 1979; N. Keizer. 'Les choix de la RFA', *Économie et statistique*, July 1978.

6 Keizer, op. cit.

7 See, for example: Centre d'Études Prospectives et d'Informations Internationales (CEPII), 'Spécialisations et adaptations face à la crise', *Economie prospective internationale*, No. 1, January 1980; G. Lafay, 'Remarques sur la compétitivité en longue periode', *Economie et statistique*, July 1978; J. Mistral, 'Compétitivité et formation de capital en longue periode', *Economie et statistique*, February 1978; Y. Barou *et al.*, 'Croissance interne et compétitivité internationale', *Economie et statistique*, November 1978; R. Boyer and P. Petit, 'Emploi et productivité dans la CEE', *Economie et statistique*, April 1980.

8 Commission of the European Communities, Report of the Group of Experts on Sectoral Analyses, *Changes in Industrial Structure in the European Economies since the Oil Crisis*, Brussels, July 1979 (the Maldague report). This was heavily influenced by French thinking.

9 Jacques Chirac wrote: 'The French Government at the moment seems fascinated by the example of West Germany.' Michel Debré recommended: 'We must inspire ourselves by the financial and economic management of Germany.' See Klaus-Peter Schmid, 'La convergence économique franco-allemande', *Projet*, April 1979.

10 M. Aglietta *et al.*, 'L'industrie française face aux contraintes de change', *Economie et statistique*, February 1980.

11 French interest in the Japanese model is not new. See, for example: R. Guillain, *Japon: troisième grand*, Paris, Seuil, 1969; C. Sautter *et al., La Planification en France et au Japon*, Paris, Institut National de la Statistique et des Etudes Economiques (INSEE), 1978 (Collections de l'INSEE No. 261, Sér. C: No. 61); C. Sautter, 'Croissance et stratégie internationale du Japon', *Economie et statistique*, February 1978. The CEPII study referred to in note 7 concluded that Japanese industry ranked first in terms of its ability to adapt to changes in world demand and in terms of its positions in the key sectors of the future, ahead of Germany and the USA. Interest in the Japanese model is also catching up in the United Kingdom; see, for example, I. C. Magaziner and T. M. Hout, *Japanese Industrial Policy*, London, Policy Studies Institute, 1980.

12 In practice, German banks play a major role in co-ordinating and implementing a *de facto* industrial policy. See: Andrew Shonfield, *Modern Capitalism*, London, Oxford University Press, 1965, ch. 12; Y.S. Hu, *National Attitudes and the Financing of Industry*, London, Political and Economic Planning (PEP), December 1975.

Relative Poverty, Convergence of Economic Performance and the Community Budget

The less-prosperous member states emphasize the convergence of economic performances or achievements in the Community. This means the convergence of income levels rather than inflation rates. There has been, however, a major difference between the case of the United Kingdom and that of the other less prosperous countries (Italy, Ireland, and Greece at present, who will be joined by Portugal and Spain when the present round of enlargement is concluded). In the British case, convergence got tangled up with the problem of net contributions to the Community budget, whereas the other less prosperous member states (and some not so poor ones) have been calling for a greater emphasis on Community structural and redistributive policies.

Convergence/divergence of income levels

Gross domestic product (GDP) per capita is the indictor most often used for comparing income levels and standards of living. GDPs expressed in different national currencies have, however, to be expressed in a common denominator. This can be done in two ways: at market exchange rates, or at purchasing-power parities (PPPs). The use of market exchange rates can· distort the comparison by accentuating the differences between countries. In the relatively rich countries, goods and services, particularly those that are not internationally traded, tend to be more expensive so that a GDP per capita that is x per cent higher than in another country (measured at market exchange rates) does not imply a standard of living that is x per cent higher. Moreover, market exchange rates are subject to rapid changes, especially since the breakdown in the early 1970s of the Bretton Woods system of fixed exchange rates. Yet a currency revaluation of x per cent does not entail a *pro tanto* increase in the standard of living. To try to overcome these difficulties, statisticians have calculated purchasing-power parities. Yet there is a fundamental methodological problem here, in addition to the difficulty of gathering comparable data. The calculation of PPPs (or, what amounts to the same thing, the comparison of GDP volumes) must implicitly take a certain structure of production and consumption as given, as the frame of reference. This is necessary in order to allocate weights to individual prices or quantities so that they can be aggregated. But the structure of production, consumption, and tastes are not uniform from country to country. If, for example, housing is considered relatively more important in one country, and food in another, how can this be properly taken account of in adding housing and food to reach a statistical aggregate? Thus, comparisons based on PPPs reduce some of the distortions inherent in comparisons based on market exchange rates, but are far from being flawless. They reduce the extent of disparities between countries, but are not likely to reverse them.

There is another major difficulty in comparing income levels across countries. Depending on the country, a significant part of total economic activity, referred to as the black or underground economy, is not captured by GDP statistics. Since the relative size of the black economy varies from country to country, GDP per capita cannot be relied upon to indicate correct ratios between countries. To take a particular example, it is often estimated that the relative Italian position would look 10 to 20 per cent better if proper account were taken of its underground economy.

Whether, and to what extent, living standards have converged also depends on the time period under examination and on whether one is looking at all the countries in the sample or concentrating on a few problem countries. Trying to look at nine countries simultaneously involves the construction of complicated measures, such as Theil's index of inequality, and may mask rather than elucidate the problems facing the less prosperous countries. For this reason, I shall look at individual countries in turn.

For more than a century, the UK economy has consistently displayed a slower rate of growth than most other West European economies[1]. As long as income levels were higher in the United Kingdom, however, this lower ability to grow did not seem to matter. Indeed, the higher growth rates of the other countries only served to close the gap between British and continental income levels, i.e. to bring about convergence of income levels. Convergence turned into divergence, however, when in the course of the 1960s, the six (except Italy) successively overtook the UK level and *still* persisted with their higher growth rates. This became a Community problem when the United Kingdom joined the EEC in January 1973. From a GDP per capita that was, at market exchange rates, 17 per cent higher than the average[2] for the Nine in 1960, the UK position slipped to the point where it was 11 per cent lower than the average in 1970 and 28 per cent lower in 1977 (though with the recent recovery in the value of sterling the gap has narrowed somewhat to 24 per cent in 1979). In terms of PPPs, the picture is less unfavourable, but the UK position still worsened from 112 per cent of the average for the Nine in 1960 to 92 per cent in 1977 and 91 per cent in 1979 (*Table 4.1*).

Table 4.1 *EEC countries: gross domestic product per capita as percentage of the EEC average (purchasing-power parities)*

	1960	1970	1976	1977	1979[1]
Belgium	99	102	109	109	108
Denmark	113	121	112	119	116
France	100	106	113	113	112
Federal Republic of Germany	118	116	118	119	118
Ireland	59	61	61	62	61
Italy	69	76	73	72	77
Luxembourg	n.a.	127	n.a.	110	111
Netherlands	104	107	107	108	103
United Kingdom	112	97	93	92	91

1. Estimated.
Source: EC Commission, *European Economy*, November 1978 and November 1979.

The story of Italy is radically different. After the war, Italy started at a very low level, with a per capita income of around US$290 in 1950, but the 1950s and the first half of the 1960s were the years of the Italian miracle. During much of this period, Italian GDP and exports grew at rates that surpassed those of France and Germany, and compared favourably with those of Japan. Italian living standards converged towards those of its EEC partners. Italian GDP per capita, at market exchange rates, rose from 60 per cent of the average for the Nine in 1960 to reach 80 per cent in 1968. In 1969, however, the social tensions that had underlain the phenomenal growth erupted, massive strikes broke out in the 'hot autumn', and 37 million working days were lost (compared with 9 million the previous year). Italian GDP per capita fell to 70 per cent of the average in 1969, and Italy's relative position has never recovered since then. Largely because of the depreciation of the lira, it fell to 56 per cent in 1977 and 1978 before recovering slightly to 61 per cent in 1979. Measured in PPPs, however, the Italian position rose from 69 per cent of the average in 1960 to 76 per cent in 1970, and after falling has recovered to 77 per cent in 1979.

As for Ireland, there has been a small improvement in its relative position measured in PPPs, from 59 per cent of the average for the Nine in 1960 to around 61 per cent in recent years.

Apart from the United Kingdom, the largest shifts in relative positions concern France and Luxembourg. In PPPs, French GDP per capita rose from 100 per cent of the average in 1960 to 106 per cent in 1970 and 113 per cent in 1977, while Luxembourg's fell from 127 per cent in 1970 to 110 per cent in 1977. Within the original Six, minus Italy but plus Denmark, there appears to be a convergence of income levels. Between 1960 and 1979, differences between France, Germany, the Benelux countries and Denmark have been markedly reduced, in PPP terms. According to E. C. Hallett[3], 'this had led in effect to the emergence of a two-tier Community as far as income levels are concerned, with the upper tier consisting of the countries listed above and the lower tier consisting of Ireland, Italy and the UK. The gap between the upper and lower tier appears to be widening. Measured in PPPs, the upper tier comprises a band from about 105 per cent of Community average GDP per capita to about 120 per cent.

What will be the impact of the second enlargement of the Community to include Greece, Spain and Portugal? It is quite true that the inclusion of these countries will widen the degree of disparity of income levels within the EEC. However, because of their higher growth rates – higher than those of existing member states – there has been convergence of their levels towards the EEC level. As a percentage of the Community average (at market exchange rates), the GDP per capita of Greece and Spain rose from 36.0 and 33.2 respectively in 1960 to 43.8 and 58.2 in 1979. Portugal's relative position rose from 24 per cent of the average in 1960 to 33 per cent in 1974 but has since fallen to 22.5 per cent in 1979. In the future, convergence of living standards will obviously depend on the acceding countries maintaining higher growth rates than the Community average.

Calls for the convergence of economic performance

The less prosperous member states (the United Kingdom, Italy and Ireland) have been pressing the Community to promote the 'convergence of economic performances or achievements', which means the reduction of income disparities between countries and regions through Community policies and expenditures, such as the regional and social policies, which have come to be labelled 'structural' policies. These demands are based on the objectives of the Community, which are enshrined in the Treaty of Rome establishing the EEC. The preamble of the Treaty states:

'[The signatories] ... desirous of strengthening the unity of their economies and of ensuring their harmonious development by reducing the disparities existing between the various regions and the backwardness of the less favoured regions ... have decided to create a European Economic Community. ...'

And Article 2 states:

'It shall be the task of the Community, by establishing a Common Market and progressively approximating the economic policies of Member States, to promote throughout the Community a harmonious development of economic activities, a continuous and balanced expansion, an increased stability, an accelerated raising of the standard of living and closer relations between its Member States.'

The debate between the less prosperous and the more prosperous member states and the question as to whether the Community can and should promote a genuine convergence of economic performance are analysed in Chapter 9. At this stage, however, it is necessary to clear up the confusion which has been generated by the British budgetary problem and to inquire into the links between the convergence and budget issues.

Convergence and the British budgetary problem

Ever since the United Kingdom reapplied for Community membership in 1970, the two issues of convergence and the budgetary problem have always been tangled up. The links between the two, however, are not purely logical, and are best understood in a historical, tactical sense. (The following analysis is based on discussions with senior officials in Brussels.)

In 1969, the Community of Six finally agreed on the Own Resources system of providing for the Community budget. Conceptually, this marked a radical departure from the traditional intergovernmental approach, in which the common budget is financed by national contributions. Under the Own Resources system, the contributions to the Community budget (the levies on agricultural imports from outside the Community, the duties on imports of other goods from third countries, and a certain percentage of a harmonized value-added tax base which should not exceed 1 per cent and which is so calculated as to bridge the gap between Community expenditures and Community revenues from levies and duties) are subject to automatic assessment and are regarded as belonging to the Community domain (e.g. because it is a free-trade area with a common commercial policy) rather than as contributions from the member states. President Pompidou had insisted on such an institutional anchor in order to guarantee the definitive and irreversible character of the Common Agricultural Policy, in return for allowing the United Kingdom to apply for EEC membership[4], which the other Five desired.

When the United Kingdom began its application in 1970, it already foresaw a budgetary problem (because, *inter alia*, of its dependence on imports from third countries). The perception was in terms of gross contributions rather than net contributions (i.e. gross contributions minus receipts from the Community budget), probably because of the even greater difficulty of forecasting the pattern and geographical distribution of Community expenditures in five or ten years' time than of projecting contributions to the Community budget. The United Kingdom secured a promise from the Commission that, if unacceptable situations should arise, 'the very survival of the Community would demand that the institutions find equitable solutions'. This declaration, which was reproduced in the British Government's White Paper of July 1971[5], was not, however, incorporated into the Treaty of Accession, but took the form merely of being adopted in the Commission's minutes of the negotiations. The reason was that, in the membership negotiations, the United Kingdom was *demandeur* and the legal basis of the entire negotiations was an acceptance by all of the *acquis communautaire*; the negotiations could only be about derogations from the Community rules during the transitional period of membership and about the length of the transitional period. This was not only clearly recognized by the UK Government but also clearly stated in the White Paper of July 1971[5]:

> 'From the outset the Government recognized, as did their predecessors, that it would not be possible to seek to make fundamental alterations in the system of providing funds for the Community. The existing members had finally agreed this system among themselves early in 1970 only after considerable difficulty and regarded it as an essential part of the process of "completing" the Community envisaged in the Hague communiqué. The negotiations have therefore been directed to finding a method to enable us gradually to adapt to the Community system over a period of years, without placing an undue burden on our economy.'

In the event, the United Kingdom secured a transitional period of five years for its budgetary contributions, plus a further period of two years during which the increase in its contributions would be limited.

The British Government therefore moved on to the convergence tack, in an attempt to increase Community expenditures in the United Kingdom to offset the country's gross contributions. At one of their bilateral meetings in 1972, Mr Edward Heath, then Prime Minister, obtained President Pompidou's agreement to the idea of a European Regional Development Fund, which was then launched on the Community stage. In the subsequent Community debate, however, there was a great deal of confusion between regional policy and budgetary considerations. Then came the Yom Kippur War and the first oil crisis of 1973–4, which radically altered the economic prospects facing the Community. France, feeling vulnerable, decided to press for a large share of the regional fund, thereby vitiating the UK design. The point, to put it simply, was that, when all member states are entitled to a share in ERDF spending, then the ERDF ceases to be a suitable channel for dealing with the British budgetary problem, since Britain has to pay its share in financing any increase in the Community budget and hence in the ERDF. The net gain to the United Kingdom from the ERDF results from the difference between UK share in total ERDF expenditure and its share in financing increases in the total Community budget. According to Commission calculations made in October 1979, with a UK share of 27 per cent in total ERDF expenditure and of 17.36 per cent in financing any increase in the Community budget, even a ninefold increase in total ERDF expenditure (by 5000 million EUAs) would have reduced Britain's net contribution in 1980 by less than a third. Yet the chances of such an increase in the ERDF must be rated as rather remote when one recalls that the total Community budget for 1980 amounted to 15,683 million EUAs.

The next act in the play was the renegotiation of UK membership of the Community by the Labour Government, which had succeeded Mr Heath's government in spring 1974. The renegotiations swung the budgetary terms back to the centre of British demands, and Mr Harold Wilson, then British Prime Minister, was reported to have been prepared to drop the regional fund in order to concentrate on the budget issue.

The result was the establishment in 1976 of a Financial Mechanism[6] which would serve, under certain circumstances, to reduce the United Kingdom's gross contribution. It is significant that its criteria made explicit reference to economic divergence in income levels. The member state that is 'asking for a refund of part of its excessive payments to the Community budget (excessive in relation to its share of total Community GDP) must at the same time be *diverging* from the EEC average in terms of income levels: its per capita GDP (at market exchange rates) has to be 15 per cent or more below the Community average and, at the same time, its growth rate of per capita GDP has to be less than 120 per cent of the Community average. If the growth rate exceeds 120 per cent of the average, the presumption must be that the gap in income levels is gradually being closed through a higher rate of growth, i.e. that convergence in income levels is taking place. Thus the concept of the convergence of 'economic performance or achievements' was beginning to make headway in the Community.

As it turned out, the Financial Mechanism failed to solve the British budgetary problem, the main reason being that the mechanism concerned gross contributions to the Community budget, while the problem proved to be the size of the United Kingdom's *net* contributions, largely as a result of insufficient Community expenditures in the United Kingdom as is shown in the appendix to this chapter. (The Financial Mechanism was also assorted with upper ceilings on the amount of refunds, and with balance-of-payments conditions that hampered the United Kingdom now that it was benefiting from the flow of North Sea oil.)

Was this focus on gross contributions the result of an oversight on the part of the renegotiating Labour Government, or was it a reflection of the weakness of the United Kingdom's bargaining power? I am inclined to think that it was a bit of both. Acceptance of the Financial Mechanism was probably based on an assessment of what was attainable under the circumstances. It should be remembered that the concept of *juste retour* (between what a member state pays into and receives from the Community budget) was still widely regarded as anti-Community and that to have raised the question of *net* contributions would have gone against the doctrine of Own Resources. The British feared a steep rise in UK gross contributions after the transitional period had ended. The Community budget is an extremely complicated system, and the Commission had not until then published figures about member states' contributions and receipts, on grounds of Community principle. It was therefore very difficult to forecast the size of the UK contributions and receipts in relation to those of the other Eight. It was also hoped that the CAP could be reformed and that this would permit more spending on other Community policies from which the United Kingdom stood to benefit.

In the event, while the transitional period during which the United Kingdom's budgetary contributions were limited ran out, it proved almost impossible to reform the CAP, and British attempts to impose a freeze on CAP prices led to hostile conflicts between the United Kingdom and the other member states. Meanwhile, the debate swung back to the convergence issue, in connection with the proposed launching of the EMS. Concurrent studies were undertaken to see how the weaker member states could be helped to join and remain in the EMS. In these studies, the budgetary contributions, receipts and net positions of each member state were shown for the first time by the Commission, which also calculated what the United Kingdom net contributions would have been if there had been no transitional limitations. These figures revealed the magnitude of the British problem: despite a lower gross contribution than that of the Federal Republic of Germany, the United Kingdom had overtaken it as the Community's largest *net* contributor in 1979 (if MCAs – monetary compensatory amounts – are attributed to the exporting member state) and, without the introduction of a new compensating mechanism, would have become by far the largest net contributor in 1980 (whichever way the MCAs are attributed). All this was without any foreseeable prospect of an improvement in the situation and despite the fact that the United Kingdom was the third poorest member state.

It was in this context that Mrs Thatcher, who had become Prime Minister in spring 1979, decided to press vigorously and (some would say) stridently for a 'broad balance' between UK gross contributions and receipts. Despite the fact that Commission papers on the subject often carried the title 'Convergence and Budgetary Issues', convergence was not really on, as far as Britain was concerned. The United Kingdom had decided not to join, at least for the time being, the exchange-rate mechanism of the EMS (although it did join the reserve pooling arrangements – see appendix to Chapter 8) and hence could not expect to benefit from the special measures under the EMS for the less prosperous participants; the interest-relief grants would in any case have been too small to make a real difference to the United Kingdom's net budgetary problem. As noted earlier, the Commission's calculations also showed that, even if the regional fund were increased fivefold or tenfold, the United Kingdom's budgetary problem would remain. In the course of 1979, therefore, the ideological camouflage of convergence was dropped and the UK case was presented in straight cash terms – though it was still argued that large net contributions from one of the poorest member states were a major factor in causing divergence.

The bargaining position of the United Kingdom was an amalgam of weakness and strength. Whatever the reduction in the UK net contributions, it would mean a *pro rata* increase in payments or decrease in receipts for each of the other member states, so that Mrs Thatcher succeeded in uniting the Eight against her demands. The United Kingdom also lost its only potential ally, Italy, when Commission figures revealed that, contrary to expectations, Italy had become a net recipient from the Community budget. Also, Mrs Thatcher's intransigence apparently caused much consternation, shock and ill will (she openly rejected various proposals by her partners at two successive meetings of the European Council, in Dublin in November 1979 and in Venice in spring 1980). Nevertheless, the United Kingdom's ruthless determination appears to have been a major factor in bringing about some concessions. The British, moreover, played a trump card, the veto on CAP price increases, increases which the French Government badly needed for domestic political and electoral reasons. The French threatened to adopt national measures to protect their farmers' incomes, but these measures would have been quite expensive; moreover, such a move ran the risk of breaking up the CAP, from which France still derives considerable benefits, and there was little support for such action from the other member states. The United Kingdom also made threatening noises about withholding its VAT payments to the Community budget.

The Federal Republic of Germany and the other six member states had always been more sympatic and receptive to the British case than France, and recognized that the situation was unstable and untenable and could not last much longer. The Federal Republic has wider international reasons for wanting Britain to remain in the European Community. During the 1974–5 UK renegotiations, the United Kingdom contribution to Western defence, in particular through the British Army of the Rhine, must have been an important consideration in German thinking. Now, in 1980, the international situation was dominated by the Soviet military intervention in Afghanistan and its aftermath, and, as Herr Klaus von Dohnanyi, the German negotiator at the meeting of the Council of Ministers which finally reached agreement on the British problem, declared[7]:

> 'Britain's negotiating methods may be open to criticism in certain details, but in fact no Government would have been able to resist the internal political pressure for a cut in the budget contribution. On the contrary, the delay in reaching a decision in the Community has already aroused dangerous anti-European emotions in Britain. The Federal Republic of Germany has a vital interest in a Britain which belongs – and wants to belong – to the EEC.'

At the end of May 1980, agreement was reached by the Council of Foreign Ministers in Brussels. Roughly speaking, the budgetary refund offered to the United Kingdom went half-way between the broad balance that Mrs Thatcher had originally demanded, and the 'half loaf' that she had scornfully rejected – British net contributions were to be reduced by 34 per cent (in relation what it would otherwise have had to pay, according to Commission estimates) in 1980 and 1981, with a presumption that this would continue thereafter if the problem has not been resolved by then 'by means of structural changes'[8].

The implications of the budget settlement for the Community are discussed in Chapter 9. The sheer scale of the settlement is noteworthy. The reductions in the United Kingdom's net contributions are to be 1175 million EUAs in 1980 and 1410 million EUAs in 1981, a total of 2585 million EUAs or US$3670 million for the two years. These figures compare with total forecast regional-fund expenditure of less than 700 million EUAs in 1980. Meanwhile, with the continuous increase in CAP spending, the Community budget is expected to hit the 1 per cent VAT ceiling in a couple of years' time. There is no precedent to determine how the different Community expenditure commitments will then be met. One view is that there will not be much money left for the British settlement. However, expenditure for the British settlement has the status of an 'obligatory' expenditure, on a par with CAP spending. Legally speaking, therefore, CAP expenditures do not take precedence over the British settlement. In fact there will be a political crisis in the Community, when the 1 per cent ceiling is reached, which will call for a political solution; the future of the British budgetary settlement will form a part of that overall political solution.

According to the May 1980 agreement, the budgetary funds to the United Kingdom are not described as refunds, but as payments. These payments are to be made by adapting and relaxing the Financial Mechanism and by means of special Community expenditure in the United Kingdom for 'structural' purposes. Formally at least, a link has been preserved with the promotion of convergence (through structural measures).

Divergent performance and the British problem

There is an underlying link between the British budgetary problem (and the problem of the ambivalent attitude of the United Kingdom towards Europe) and the convergence/divergence problem. When the United Kingdom applied for EEC membership, it knew that there would be static costs of membership in terms of budgetary contributions and higher costs of food imports, but the hope was that these would be more than compensated for by the dynamic effects of membership. If the UK economy had grown faster than it did since the beginning of membership in 1973, if UK income levels had converged towards the EEC average level, the chances are that the budgetary problem would have assumed a less salient importance. The British people might have been more convinced of the economic benefits of membership, and the country would have been more capable of paying into the Community budget. Whether because of the uncompetitiveness of British industry or the advent of a world economic recession in the wake of the 1973–4 oil crisis (which cut average EEC growth rates by half), the perceived failure of the dynamic effects to materialize through convergence must be a major factor in the continuing problem of negative British attitudes towards membership. (This is not to say, however, that the poor UK economic performance is due to EEC membership.)

Summary and conclusions

As regards income levels measured in PPPs the major divergence concerns the United Kingdom. This has been due to the persistence of a lower British rate of growth after the UK level had been overtaken by other countries. Despite interruptions caused by political and social unrest, Italian living standards at PPPs have, during the last twenty years, been converging towards the Community average. Because of a major shift in France's relative position (at PPPs), there is also convergence towards a much narrower band between France, the Federal Republic of Germany and the Benelux countries, which may be considered to constitute an upper tier within the Community. Whether or not the Mediterranean countries can converge depends on their maintaining their past record of high growth rates. To say all this is not to deny that significant disparities will remain.

The less prosperous member states emphasize the 'convergence of economic peformance or achievements', which means the reduction of income-level disparities through Community 'structural' policies and expenditures. In the case of the United Kingdom, however, the convergence and budget issues have always been tangled up. The link between the two is not purely logical, and is to be understood in a historical and political context. Depending on circumstances and the degree of success encountered, the emphasis in British arguments and negotiating tactics in the Community has alternated between calls for convergence and more direct demands on its budgetary contributions. The focus has swung from the regional fund to the Financial Mechanism to convergence and finally to a demand for broad balance. There is also an underlying link in that, if British economic performance had been better and British income levels had converged towards the EEC average, the budgetary problem (and the problem of Britain's ambivalent attitude towards membership of the European Community) would have assumed much less prominence. This is not to say, however, that the poor economic performance of the United Kingdom is due to the EEC.

The Origins of the British Budgetary Problem

How was it that the United Kingdom became such a large net contributor to the Community budget, while the other less prosperous member states (Italy and Ireland) were net recipients? In simple terms, this resulted from the interaction between British economic structures and the mechanisms of the CAP and of the Community budget.

Of the Nine, the United Kingdom is unique in having the smallest agricultural sector in relation to the size of its economy. This is the result of history and different policies adopted over the last hundred years or more. In Britain, the enclosure movement started in the sixteenth century; the repeal of the Corn Laws (which had protected agriculture against imports) took place in 1846, and a long period of free trade and cheap imported food from abroad and in particular from continents outside Europe resulted in a shrinking in the size of the agricultural sector that, despite some increase through government support during the two world wars and since the end of the Second World War, today represents only 2.3 per cent of GDP at factor cost and 2.7 per cent of total employment[9]. The other European nations had never allowed free trade and the decline of their agricultural sectors to go so far. In the 1880s, when technical progress in transportation had made an immense increase in exports of cheap grain from America and Russia to Europe possible at lower and lower prices, France, Germany and Italy introduced tariff protection for agriculture, a tradition which has survived until today. Denmark and the Netherlands adhered more or less to free trade, but instead of following a policy of pure *laissez-faire* as in Britain, adopted active measures to encourage their agricultures to adapt to the new conditions and to shift from crops to livestocks and (in the Netherlands) to fruits and vegetables. Both countries became strong exporters of agricultural produce to the British and German markets[10]. As a result, all the other countries had and still have a relatively larger agriculture than Britain. In 1968, for example, agriculture represented about 15 per cent of total employment in the Six, and despite some rapid decline since, it still represents 8 per cent today in the Community of Nine.

As is well known, the CAP uses prices (which are guaranteed within certain limits and which are protected from the world market by a system of variable levies) to support farmers' incomes. In terms of administrative simplicity as well as budgetary costs, this system is much more suitable for countries with large numbers of farmers than is the deficiency-payment system which was applied in the United Kingdom. There is no need, as in the deficiency-payment system, to make dozens of payments each to tens or hundreds of thousands of farmers (some of whom may make a habit of cheating); the consumer pays the higher prices without any government budgetary intervention; and it was thought (alas, wrongly) that, barring massive surpluses, the import levies would largely suffice to pay for the costs of surplus disposal and export restitution.

The open-ended commitment to purchase surplus production for most products covered by the CAP has meant that EAGGF spending in a country (counted as a receipt from the Community budget) depends on the amount of surplus production sold into intervention agencies in that country and on exports to third countries which qualify for export restitutions. This means that EAGGF spending is likely to vary positively with a country's agricultural output, degree of self-sufficiency, exports to third countries, etc.

Table 4.2 *UK net contribution to the Community budget, 1980*[1]

	£ million	As percentage of Community total
1. UK gross contribution	2075	20.5
2. UK gross contribution if in line with UK share of Community GDP	1621	16.0
3. UK receipts[2]	855	8.5
4. UK net contribution (1 − 3)	1209	
Of which		*As percentage of total net contribution*
5. Excess gross contribution (1 − 2)	454	37.5
6. Deficient receipts (2 − 3)	755	62.5

1. If the budgetary settlement had not intervened.
2. MCAs on exports to the United Kingdom are attributed to the exporters.
Source: Commission of the ECs, *Reference Paper on Budgetary Questions*, Brussels, September 1979 (COM(79)462).

On all these counts, the United Kingdom compares badly with the Eight. The relatively high British net contribution to the Community budget is due more to insufficient receipts than to excessive gross contribution. If in 1980 the budgetary settlement had not intervened, and using the United Kingdom's share in total Community GDP (at market exchange rates) as the norm, it has been calculated[11] that 62.5 per cent of the UK net contribution would represent insufficient receipts compared with the norm and 37.5 per cent excessive gross contribution (*Table 4.2*). Thus two-thirds of the British problem would have been due to the predominance of the CAP in the Community budget and the size of UK agriculture. The remainder, the excessive contributions to the Community's Own Resources (customs duties, import levies, and VAT), results from the fact that the United Kingdom imports relatively more from third countries and that consumption and imports (which attract VAT) represent a larger proportion of GDP.

44   *Relative poverty*

1 This secular tendency is well documented by economic historians. See I. Svennilson, *Growth and Stagnation in the European Economy*, Geneva, United Nations Economic Commission for Europe, 1954. For a more recent statement, see the article by D. T. Jones in the *National Institute Economic Review*, August 1976. For a comprehensive analysis recently completed, see Keith Pavitt (ed.), *Technological Innovation and British Economic Performance*, London, Macmillan, 1980.

2 The Community average is the total Community GDP divided by total Community population.

3 E. C. Hallett, 'Economic Divergence in the Community: A Survey of the Evidence', in W. Wallace (ed.), *Economic Divergence and the European Community* (forthcoming).

4 This is candidly admitted by French scholars. See various chapters in Joël Rideau *et al.* (ed.), *La France et les Communautés européennes*, Paris, 1975, in particular pp. 65, 366, 373 and 374.

5 United Kingdom, *The UK and the European Communities*, HMSO, July 1971 (Cmnd 4715).

6 Council Regulation (EEC) No. 1172/76 of 17 May 1976 (*Official Journal of the ECs*, 20 May 1976). M. R. Emmerson and T. W. K. Scott, 'The financial mechanism in the budget of the European Community: the hard core of the British "renegotiations" of 1974–75', *Common Market Law Review*, May 1977.

7 Klaus von Dohnanyi, Minister of State in the Foreign Ministry, 'An Opportunity for Europe', reprinted in *Report from the Federal Republic of Germany*, London, German Embassy, 11 June 1980.

8 See the full text of the proposed compromise solution, reproduced in *The Times*, 31 May 1980.

9 The figures are for 1978, and are to be found in the European Commission's *1979 Report on the Agricultural Situation in the Community*, Brussels, January 1980.

10 See Michael Tracy, *Agriculture in Western Europe*, London, 1964.

11 Commission of the European Communities, *Reference Paper on Budgetary Questions*, Brussels, September 1979 (COM(79)462).

Community Policies

The emphasis in Part One was primarily on the perceptions and interests of the member states of the Community: Part Two now turns to the consequences and implications of economic divergence for Community policies. A number of major policy areas have been selected for study because of their importance and centrality to the European Community. As stated before, the purpose is not to provide an exhaustive technical treatment of these policies for their own sake, but to use the case studies to illustrate our general themes.

It will be seen that the concepts of divergence and convergence can contribute to a better understanding of European affairs by shedding a different light on developments from those suggested by the theory of integration and the approach of institutional politics. It will also be shown that what is crucial, in terms of its policy consequences and political significance, is the divergence of perceived national interests; where divergent economic developments have been important, it is through perceived national interests that they have had an impact.

Agri-monetary Issues in the Common Agricultural Policy[1]

One of the most important and prevalent reasons for regarding economic divergence as a major problem for the Community is the argument that it threatens the *acquis communautaire*. In the case of the CAP, 'our most highly developed and most integrated form of common action'[2], the argument is that divergent inflation rates between member states have resulted, through the 'green money' system and the monetary compensatory amounts (MCAs), in serious distortions in the functioning of the common market in agricultural products, in a breakdown of the principle of the unity of prices, and in an increased burden for the Community budget. The theme of this chapter, however, is that it is only through a divergence of perceived national interests that divergent economic developments can cause major *political* problems to arise for the Community.

Monetary Compensatory Amounts and the agri-monetary system

Common prices under the CAP only lasted for barely two years, from 1967 to 1969. In the summer of 1969 the French franc was devalued, and in autumn of the same year the Deutschmark was officially revalued after a period of floating. Thus began an era, which has not completely ended today, of MCAs and 'green' exchange rates, which were at first devised as strictly temporary measures in order to reconcile the principle of the unity of prices under the CAP and the temporary (so it was hoped) differences in price levels between member states.

The MCA system has become so complex that a complete treatise would be required to do full justice to the subject. At the obvious risk of over-simplification, it may be said that MCAs are introduced or increased on a member state's trade in CAP products when its currency is devalued or revalued but when, for national political or economic reasons, it is reluctant to adjust its 'green' rate (used to convert common prices expressed in units of account into national prices) immediately to market rate changes. If, for example, initially 1 unit of account equals 4 German marks (DM4), then a product for which a common price of 100 units of account has been fixed in Brussels would sell in Germany for DM400. But if the DM is revalued by 10 per cent, so that one unit of account equals only DM3636, and the green mark is immediately aligned on the market or 'spot' value of the DM, the same product would sell for only DM363.6 compared with DM400 previously. In these circumstances, the German Government may well decide that the fall in farmers' incomes that this implies is politically unacceptable, and should be postponed by maintaining the green mark at its previous value. Similarly, for a country with a depreciating currency (at times, France, Italy, the United Kingdom), immediate alignment of the green rate on the 'spot' rate would imply a rise in farm prices, which the country may want to delay because of its anti-inflation programme or because it wants to protect consumers.

The difference between green and market rates means, however, that at market rates the lower French farm prices would enable French farmers to undersell their EEC competitors, and particularly the Germans (or that the French farmers could obtain higher intervention prices in Germany than in France); whereas French, German, Dutch and Danish farmers would have to cut their prices when exporting to the United Kingdom and Italy. To prevent these distortions to the CAP principle of unity of prices, MCAs were instituted as a device to bridge the gap between green and market rates of exchange, the intention being that these should be temporary devices to give time for adjustment. In the case of a country with a depreciating currency, *negative* MCAs act as export levies and import subsidies, so that the country's agricultural exports do not gain in price competitiveness and its EEC partners can continue to export to its market. Conversely, with a country with an appreciating currency, *positive* MCAs act as export subsidies and import levies. The MCAs are calculated by multiplying the support price for each commodity by the percentage difference between green and market exchange rates.

For the United Kingdom and Italy, both net food-importing countries which have had depreciating currencies, negative MCAs have kept food-import prices below what they would otherwise have been, given the CAP regime. In certain periods between 1976 and 1979, negative MCAs reached peaks of 20 to 30 per cent for the United Kingdom and Italy (but subsequent devaluations of the green pound and the rising value of the pound on the foreign exchange market turned the United Kingdom into a positive MCA country in 1980). It was not these deviations from the principle of uniform prices, however, that provoked a major political crisis in the Community. Other member states and the Commission may have complained, but these complaints were not really serious as long as the British and Italian markets remained fully accessible for the farmers of the other countries. Nor was it the fact that, because of the bookkeeping methods adopted and the trade flows, MCAs came to account for some 10 to 15 per cent of total spending of the European Agricultural Guidance and Guarantee Fund (EAGGF). In fact, EAGGF expenditure, expressed in EUAs, increased by 43 per cent in

1978 and 12 per cent in 1979 without in itself triggering a major political row.

What caused a serious problem for the Community, in a political sense, was a divergence and conflict of national interests between France and Germany, which erupted in connection with the coming into operation of the European monetary system (EMS).

The rise of German agricultural power[3]

In a speech in Munich on 9 March 1978, Mr Christopher Tugendhat, EEC Commissioner responsible for budgetary affairs, declared:

> 'By far the greater part of CAP expenditure arises in those sectors where we have the largest surpluses. ... Many people are surprised to learn that the lion's share of these surpluses is now held in Germany.'

Between 1976 and 1977, Germany accounted for 33 per cent of the increase in EAGGF spending, Guarantee Section[4], compared with 14 per cent for France[5]. Between 1977 and 1978, calculated according to Commission data[6], Germany accounted for 60 per cent of the increase in Guarantee spending, compared with 7 per cent for France. Germany's share of total EAGGF Guarantee spending rose from 15.7 per cent in 1976 to 18.7 per cent in 1977 and 26.7 per cent in 1978. The percentages for France were 25.3 per cent, 19.7 per cent and 16.7 per cent.

If we take dairy products, which now account for more than 35 per cent of total EAGGF spending, Guarantee Section, and more than 27 per cent of the total Community budget, available figures from the European Commission[7] indicate that, as of 1 April 1978, Germany accounted for 73 per cent of the Community's butter stocks (in tonnes) and 67 per cent of its total skimmed milk powder stocks (also in tonnes), up from 66 per cent and 64 per cent respectively a year before.

The German explanation is that intervention stocks are high because other countries' farmers prefer to sell their surpluses to intervention buying agencies in Germany because they receive speedier payments or higher prices. In any case, this line of reasoning, valid through it may be regarding surplus stocks, fails to take account of the increasing German share in total EEC agricultural output and trade.

According to Commission statistics[8], between 1970 and 1976 the Federal Republic of Germany increased its share of total EEC gross value added in agriculture from 18.7 per cent to 19.5 per cent, while France's share decreased from 30.1 per cent to 28.5 per cent. Between 1973 and 1976, the increase in exports of agricultural products to other EEC countries was 80 per cent for Germany and 40 per cent for France. If one distrusts these general figures because of the well-known techincal problems of aggregation (exchange rates, price levels, etc.), one may turn to data at the individual product level. Of twelve major products examined by the Commission[9], Germany's share of intra-Community exports, taking the period from the beginning of the 1970s to 1976 or 1977 as a whole, increased in the case of seven products, decreased in one case, and remained more or less stable for the other four products. The more remarkable increases are seen in *Table 5.1*.

Table 5.1 *Germany's share of intra-Community exports of selected farm products (percentage by weight)*

	1971	1972	1973	1974	1975	1976	1977
Wheat	0.5	0.2	3.0	3.4	2.6	6.0	10.5
Barley	1.4	3.1	4.7	3.2	2.2	4.2	4.2
Maize	1.7	1.9	2.4	3.2	3.7	6.8	7.2
Sugar	5.1	14.7	11.7	26.0	16.9	19.6	26.3
Beef and veal	9.6	10.2	15.6	14.5	15.3	15.1	15.6
Lard	21.7	21.2	21.0	27.0	24.9	28.5	29.6
Milk and fresh milk products	44.8	51.6	53.0	64.1	64.9	64.5	68.4
Butter	9.3	7.1	16.6	27.5	24.7	18.8	26.4
Chesse	13.3	13.6	15.3	16.7	17.3	18.2	20.5

Source: EEC Commission, COM(79)11, 14 March 1979.

The rise of German agricultural power is particularly striking in the case of milk (where it now accounts for two-thirds of intra-Community trade), butter, beef and sugar, all products giving rise to 'mountains' in the Community. Turning to France, between 1971 and 1977 its share of intra-Community exports of the twelve products increased in only one case (beef and veal, from 21 per cent to 23 per cent), decreased in nine cases, and remained constant for two products. There were, however, considerable fluctuations from year to year and the trend line for many products is interrupted by the impact of the drought in 1975–6.

How is it that, contrary to earlier French expectations and to textbook economic theory, which assumes two countries and two commodities, a country's comparative advantage in industry is accompanied by, or even contributes to, a comparative advantage in agriculture? The rise of German agriculture has many causes: internal demand, part-time farming, the same hard work and good organization as in industry, a comprehensive and efficient advisory service, infrastructural investments by the public authorities, especially the *Länder*, a flexible and regionalized banking and credit system, the good quality of German breads and sausages and good marketing networks both at home and abroad. Nevertheless, if we leave aside *processed* products, there is little doubt that one of the main causes of the rise of German agricultural power has been the 'distortions' in competitive conditions introduced through the agri-monetary system and MCAs.

In the French view, these have acted to the disadvantage of French agriculture in favour of German farmers, in three interrelated ways. First, the fact that farm prices are higher in Germany than in France tends to encourage farm production in Germany more than in France, as compared with a situation of uniform prices. Secondly, the increased German production is then sold into France and other EEC countries with the help of positive MCAs acting as export subsidies and financed from the Community budget, whereas French farm products are taxed when exported to Germany. Thirdly, modern agriculture is heavily dependent on purchased inputs such as soya, machines, fertilizers, energy, pesticides, construction materials and work, etc. which are bought in *real money* rather than *green money*. The cost of these inputs, relative to the prices which the farmers obtain for their products, is much lower in the Federal Republic than in France. It has been calculated that, early in 1978, a German farmer needed to produce 47.6 tonnes of wheat to buy a tractor, compared with 85 tonnes for a French farmer. Thus, compared with a situation of uniform prices for CAP products, MCAs increased the profitability of German farming relative to France, and this stimulated investment in German farming with the result that output expanded.

The rise of German agricultural power may be construed by the French as a violation of the fundamental bargain and understanding which made the establishment of the EEC possible (see the appendix to this chapter). It is true that French industry has grown considerably since the early days of the Treaty of Rome, but France may well reason that German industry is still the more powerful of the two and has a much larger share of the total EEC market and that France runs a trade deficit with the Federal Republic. In any case, the growth of German agricultural exports is considered to be abnormal in France, for Germany is not a country '*à vocation agricole*'[10].

Since the Germans cannot be expected to abandon their efficiency, French demands have centred on the 'unjustified and inexplicable' advantages, in the words of M. Raymond Barre[11], that MCAs have given to German agriculture. Moreover, MCAs are described in Community language as a distortion of competitive conditions, and it is the EEC's business to remove such distortions.

The European Monetary System and the Franco-German dispute over MCAs

It is often said that the agri-monetary distortions are due to divergent exchange-rate movements in the EEC and that monetary union is required to preserve the *acquis communautaire* that the CAP represents. This may well have been one of the motivations for President Giscard d'Estaing's sponsorship of the European Monetary System (EMS). In the autumn of 1978, the Council of Ministers decided, in principle, to apply the European

Currency Unit (ECU) to the CAP when the EMS came into force. In any case, the French decided to use the occasion of the inauguration of the EMS to press for a commitment concerning the abolition of MCAs.

On 5 December 1978, the European Council, meeting in Brussels, decided on the implementation of the EMS as from 1 January 1979. Paragraph (c) of point (6) under part A of the Council's resolution stated:

'... The European Council considers that the introduction of the EMS should not of itself result in any change in the situation obtaining prior to 1 January 1979, regarding the expression in national currencies of agricultural prices, MCAs, and all other amounts fixed for the purposes of the CAP. The European Council stresses the importance of henceforth avoiding the creation of permanent MCAs and progressively reducing present MCAs in order to re-establish the unity of prices of the CAP, giving also due consideration to price policy.'

At first, the French appeared to press for commitments on the phasing out of both new MCAs (those which would be created by divergent currency movements after the inauguration of the EMS) and old MCAs. At the meeting of the Council of Ministers (Agriculture) on 18–19 December 1978, the German Minister for Agriculture, Herr Ertl, refused to undertake a commitment to phase out, automatically and within one year, any *new* MCAs which might result from a Deutschmark revaluation. Germany, the Netherlands and the United Kingdom also opposed the fixing of a timetable for progressively dismantling *existing* MCAs. In the event, the French riposte went beyond the application of the ECU to the CAP. On 22 December, France announced that it would not approve the legal regulations which were necessary for the EMS to come into effect, on the grounds that the question of MCAs formed a whole with the EMS: the EMS could not start on 1 January 1979.

In Bonn, goverment spokesmen suggested that, at the recent Brussels European Council meeting, the dismantling of MCAs had been expressed as a wish, to be studied at the annual price fixing, and not as an objective with a binding timetable[12].

Subsequent meetings of the Council of Ministers (Agriculture) made it amply clear that the major stumbling-block in resolving the problem was Germany's reluctance to allow a fall in German farm prices expressed in DM. Short of a fall in the market value of the DM (which was highly unlikely), the only way in which Germany's positive MCAs could be dismantled was by revaluing the green mark, which would mean a drop in DM farm prices unless offset by a rise in common prices in units of account.

Phasing out France's negative MCAs was less of a problem; it required the devaluation of the green franc and hence a rise in French franc farm prices, which the government was willing to accept, despite M. Barre's anti-inflation policies. In Germany, because of the high level of prosperity, the level of food prices for consumers was not an issue, but given the large number of small farmers farm prices and incomes were a major political question. This was compounded by the domestic political situation. With a view to the general election in October 1980, the Social Democratic Party (SPD) relied on its junior coalition partner, the Free Deomcratic Party (FDP), to remain in power, while the latter perceived itself as dependent on the farm vote under the German system of proportional representation[13]. Moreover, Herr Josef Ertl, from Bavaria, the heartland of German agriculture, like the leader of the Opposition, Herr Franz Josef Strauss, was a strong personality; he had been Minister of Agriculture since 1969, and the FDP ministers in the Cabinet had formed a pact to the effect that all four would resign if only one of them were to be voted down on a vital point in the Cabinet[14].

The only way in which positive MCAs can be dismantled without reducing national farm prices is for a rise in common prices, as stated above, to compensate for the decrease which would otherwise follow the revaluation of the green mark. The German and French demands could, therefore, be satisfied simultaneously only if common agricultural prices in units of account were raised, and the increases used in strong currency countries to dismantle MCAs.

At the meeting of the Council of Ministers (Agriculture) on 5–6 March 1979, the Eight reached a gentlemen's agreement on the dismantling of *new* MCAs: these would be phased out within two years, but on condition that increases in common prices in units of account made this possible. This agreement is not a Council decision, since the United Kingdom was not party to it. There was apparently no agreement on the phasing out of existing MCAs (apart from a general statement of intent as embodied in the resolution of the European Council of 5 December 1978). Unless some secret understanding was reached, it does not appear that the French had much success: they obtained no commitments on the phasing out of existing MCAs, and only a commitment on new MCAs which is hedged with many uncertainties, since increases in common prices can be vetoed by any member state. (This is what the United Kingdom did in 1980 in order to secure a reduction in its net contribution to the Community budget.) Moreover, new MCAs were to continue to come into being *automatically* when a currency changed in value, whereas the French had hoped at one stage that the creation of new MCAs would be subject to prior authorization by the Council of Ministers. Finally, France lifted its reserves on the inauguration of the EMS, which was announced at the European Council meeting in Paris of 12–13 March.

Perspectives on the dispute

It may be worth recalling that, in 1964, Germany did accept a cut in German grain prices in order to enable the CAP to come into operation. In

December 1964, the Council of Ministers agreed, after long-drawn-out negotiations, on the common price level which would apply to cereals with effect from 1967–8. These prices, higher than French prices, were substantially lower than those payable to German producers in 1964–5 and 1965–6; for wheat DM425 per tonne against DM473; for rye DM375 against DM432.5; for barley DM365 against DM412[15]. Equalization payments to German farmers were authorized for a three-year period, with contributions from the EEC budget.

How was it that the German Government was able to accept this in 1964, despite the impending election in 1965? From the German viewpoint, the bargain was more attractive in 1964 than in 1979. In 1964, it was a question of making a once-for-all sacrifice in return for the implementation of the customs union which was limited by the funds for the establishment of the CAP. In 1979 it was a question of making a sacrifice every time the Deutschmark was revalued. Above all, however, the major difference between 1964 and 1979 must have been the increase in the Federal Republic's relative strength and power. This is not just a question of Germany regaining its traditional position as the leading industrial and economic power in Europe. It is also a question of the extent to which the Federal Republic was a *demandeur* in 1964. In the post-war period, Germany needed to regain respectability to be readmitted to the international community, and Europe was crucial in this respect; moreover, in 1964, the Common Market was still in the transitional period. Now the Federal Republic is treated as one of the leading powers in the Western Alliance, often in second place after the USA, the Common Market has long since been achieved and fully secured, and Giscardian France needs Germany economic and diplomatic support for a variety of purposes.

Summary and conclusions

One of the most important reasons for worrying about economic divergence is that it may threaten the *acquis communautaire*. In the case of the CAP, the argument is that divergences of inflation rates undermine the unity of prices, distort the conditions of competition and add a burden to the Community budget, through the MCAs that they bring about. In a political sense, however, what caused a serious political probem for the Community was a divergence of perceived national interests between France and the Federal Republic of Germany, to which the divergence of inflation rates and the MCA system contributed in a way that was not foreseen when MCAs were first introduced in 1969. Thus the crucial intervening variable between economic divergence and political developments in the EEC is the divergence and conflict of perceived national interests[16]. Economic divergence also results, over a long period of time, in a change in the distribution of power within the system, which influences the way in which a conflict is resolved.

Perspectives on the Establishment of the CAP

To assess what the future may have in store for the CAP, it is necessary to understand why it came into being. This is very different from producing economic or technical arguments which turn out to be *ex post* justifications for decisions taken on other grounds. It is true (and justifiable) that, for technical, political and social reasons, agriculture is not left to the vagaries of the 'free play of market forces' and farmers' incomes are supported by government intervention in most advanced industrial countries. The question remains why, within the EEC, this support was not left with national governments but was shifted on to the shoulders of the Community, a question which most of the technical arguments fail to address.

A prolonged and bitter struggle

The establishment of the CAP was the result of a prolonged and bitter struggle by France within the Community of Six. Perhaps the best way to convey today the essence and the flavour of this struggle for vital national interests is to quote General de Gaulle[16]:

> 'What would the very words 'European Economic Community' mean if Europe did not ensure, in the main, its food provisions from its own agricultural products, which can largely suffice? And what would France do in a system within which there will soon be no more tariffs except on its wheat, its meat, its milk, its wine and its fruits?. ... The date adopted for the achievement of the regulation which remains in suspense is the 31st of December. ... The Common Market must by then be standing, complete and assured, or else it must disappear. ...'

In other words, the reason why an agricultural common market was necessary was not because an industrial common market (progress towards which had already started) was technically impossible or inconceivable without it, but because France clearly perceived that the latter would benefit primarily Germany and the other free-trading members and that France, with the largest agricultural sector and agricultural potential in the EEC, would need to guarantee what it considered a vital national interest as a counterpart if it was to agree to proceed with the progressive implementation, in stages, of the industrial common market. The CAP was necessary to enable the common agricultural market to come into being, because all governments in the EEC of the Six supported agriculture through price supports and trade protection.

Between 1950 and 1953, France had pressed for the establishment of a 'green pool' in agricultural products in Europe, by analogy with the 'black pool' in coal and steel, but this failed because of UK opposition, among other causes. The conclusion of long-term supply contracts, notably between France and the Federal Republic of Germany, had not resulted in a major breakthrough for France. The Treaty of Rome establishing the EEC was signed in March 1957. 'Much as the dispositions concerning industry are precise and explicit, so are those which evoke agriculture vague', wrote de Gaulle[17], because 'our negotiations in 1957, carried away by the dream of a supranational Europe … did not see fit to insist that an essential French interest received satisfaction from the start. We must therefore either obtain satisfaction during the journey or liquidate the common market.' Another reason why the treaty was relatively more vague for agriculture and did not specify what was to be accomplished at successive dates as in the case of industrial products was the greater technical complexity of agricultural problems and the ignorance of the national delegations in 1957. As a result, the French delegation inserted in the Treaty a means of pressure or lever[18] which consisted in the passage from the first to the second stage of the transitional period of the Common Market at the end of four years, a passage which had to be unanimously approved 'upon a finding that the objectives specifically laid down in this Treaty for the first stage have in fact been attained in substance and that … the obligations have been fulfilled' (Article 8, paragraph 3). It could be argued that the objective of starting to establish the CAP during the first stage was implicit in Article 43, paragraphy 2[19]. De Gaulle and his Foreign Minister, M. Couve de Murville, used the lever with 'firmness and skill'.

Many writers have tended to emphasize de Gaulle's objections to the European Commission's policy of trying to increase the EEC's supranational powers in provoking the 'empty chair' crisis of 1965 (during which France was absent from meetings of Community institutions). In fact, it could be argued that what was directly at issue, namely agriculture and the financing of the CAP, was probably as important a factor. In March 1965, the Commission made proposals for the financing of the CAP, which at the same time would have increased the budgetary powers of the Commission and of the European Parliament. The Six failed to agree on the duration of the financing arrangements on 28–30 June 1965, and this (according to M. Couve de Murville) failure to reach an agreement within the foreseen delays was followed by the period of the 'empty chair'.

Although France's partners gave in, the battle was still incompletely won. The financing arrangement agreed to in July 1966 was provisional only and was valid only until 1970. Pompidou succeeded de Gaulle as President in

1969, and it was in exchange for a 'definitive' financial regulation that Pompidou agreed, at the summit meeting at The Hague in December 1969, to the enlargement of the Community to included the United Kingdom, which France's partners strongly desired.

1 See also Y.S. Hu, 'German agricultural power: the impact on France and Britain', *The World Today*, November 1979.
2 Leo Tindemans, *Report on European Union*, Brussels, 1976.
3 The word 'power' is used by French commentators. Although agricultural production in conditions of insufficient market outlets is not necessarily a sign of power, the French probably have in mind competitive and productive power.
4 The Guarantee Section represents 90 per cent or more of total EAGGF spending.
5 Commission of the European Communities, *EAGGF Financial Report* (Guarantee Section), Brussels, 1978 (COM(78)633).
6 Commission of the European Communities, *EAGGF Financial Reports Guarantee Section)*, Brussels, 1978, 1979 (COM(78)633, COM(79)596).
7 Commission of the European Communities, *Situation of the Agricultural Markets: Report 1978*, Brussels, 31 January 1979, table M13.16 (COM(79)50 final, Pt II).
8 Commission of the European Communities, *Economic Effects of the Agri-monetary System*, Brussels, 10 February 1978 (COM(78)20); new (updated) edition, 14 March 1979 (COM(79)11).
9 Wheat, barley, maize, sugar, beef and veal, pig-meat, lard, poultry-meat, eggs, milk and fresh milk products, butter, cheese.
10 *Le Monde*, 12 January 1979.
11 Speech of 4 January 1979 (*Financial Times*, 5 January 1979).
12 *Le Monde*, 31 December/1 January 1979.

13 The FDP estimated that it owed at least four of its seats to farmers' votes in Bavaria, Baden-Württemberg and Schleswig-Holstein (*The Economist*, 5 November 1977, p. 55).
14 S. Tangermann, 'Germany's position on the CAP: is it all the Germans' fault?', *Bruges Colloquium on European Agriculture*, June 1979.
15 W. Magura, *Chronik der Agrarpolitik und Agrarwirtschaft*, Hamburg, 1970. These common prices, however, still enforced an average price increse of 18 per cent in the EEC as a whole and of 30 per cent in France (see H. Priebe in H. Priebe *et al.*, *Fields of Conflict in European Farm Policy*, London, Trade Policy Research Centre, 1972).
16 Press conference, 29 July 1963 (see J.-C. Clavel and P. Collet, *L'Europe au fil des jours*, Paris, La Documentation Française (Notes et Études Documentaires 4509–10), 1979, p. 160).
17 *Mémoires d'espoir: le renouveau 1958–1962*, Paris, Plon, 1970, p. 193.
18 See Olivier Wormser, 'Politique agricole commune d'hier et d'aujourd'hui', *Politique étrangère* (n.s.), No. 1, 1979.
19 This stated: '... Within two years of the entry into force of this Treaty, the Commission shall submit proposals for working out and implementing the common agricultural policy. ... The Council shall, on a proposal from the Commission and after consulting the Assembly, acting unanimously during the first two stages and by a qualified majority thereafter, make regulations, issue directives, or take decisions.'

Bibliographical note

The literature on the CAP is vast. It constitutes a clearly demarcated area within the European literature, and tends to be characterized by a higher degree of analytical rigour, partly becuase of the contribution of economists and experts. It is useful to start with an understanding of the history of agriculture and agricultural policy in the different European countries until the 1950s; see for example, Michael Tracy, *Agriculture in Western Europe, Crisis and Adaptation since 1880*, London, Jonathan Cape, 1964; and the series in three volumes on *The Development of Agriculture in Germany and the UK*, published by the Centre for European Agricultural Studies (Ashford, Kent) in the later 1970s.

The CAP is such a complicated, controversial and multi-faceted subject (indeed minefield) that a collection of papers by those closely involved and exposing the reader to a spectrum of divergent views and technical topics may be the best starting-point; see M. Tracy and I. Hodac (eds.), *Prospects for Agriculture in the EEC*, Bruges, College of Europe, 1979. Noteworthy are the four chapters on French, British, Italian and German attitudes to the CAP. Two recent introductory books on the CAP are R. Fennell, *The CAP of the EC*, St Albans, Granada, 1980, and J. S. Marsh and P. J. Swanney, *Agriculture in the EC*, London, Allen & Unwin, 1980. For a political scientist's analysis, see W. J. Feld, 'Implementation of the EC's CAP: expectations, fears, failures', *International Organisation*, Summer 1979.

There does not as yet appear to be any detailed study of the Franco-German divergence of interests over the MCA issue except the article by Y. S. Hu cited in note 1. For a good explanation of the MCA system, see R. W. Irving and H. A. Fearn, *Green Money and the CAP*, Centre for European Agricultural Studies (Ashford, Kent), 1975. For a legalistic history of how MCAs came into being see G. Braakman, 'Monetary evolutions and the CAP', in *Common Market Law Review*, May 1978.

The papers by H. Delorme and by J. Bourrinet in J. Rideau (ed.), *La France et les Communautés européennes*, Paris, Librairie Générale de Droit et de Jurisprudence, 1975, and more recently, L. P. Mahé and M. Roudet, 'La politique agricole française et l'Europe verte: impasse ou révision?', *Economie rurale*, No. 135, 1980, argue that France is not benefiting as much from the CAP as is often thought. The need to renegotiate the CAP is postulated in: Commissariat Général du Plan, *L'Europe: les vingt prochaines années*, Paris, La Documentation Française, 1980.

The reading on the inter-country transfers engendered by the CAP is treated in Chapter 9 of this book.

The Common Commercial Policy

One of the fundamental motivations for European integration has been the desire to restore to a united Europe the power and influence that its individual nations had lost in a world dominated by the superpowers. In no field has this been achieved to a higher extent than in the Common Commercial Policy (CCP), so that, *vis-à-vis* the outside world on trade matters, the member states speak not only with one voice but through one single channel, the Commission. The CCP is also the indispensable under-pinning of European Political Co-operation (EPC) in foreign policy.

This chapter, which continues the themes of the last one, looks at how the CCP is affected by economic divergence and at how the divergent needs and interests of different member states can be satisfied by a common policy. It hardly needs repeating that the aim in this chapter is not to provide a comprehensive account of the European Community's trade and industry, or of its commercial and industrial policies.

Fears of disintegration

The prevailing fear in Community circles is that economic divergence between strong and weak economies (in the sense not only of disparities but also of an increase, over time, in the extent of the disparities and hence in the extent of the relative failure of the weak economies) may combine with the world economic recession (now in its eighth year and showing few signs of coming to an end) to provoke unilateral protectionist measures by the weaker economies. Such measures could have a snowball effect and under-mine both the CCP and the Common Market.

The weaker countries might suffer from competition both from their EEC partners and from third countries (in particular the new industrial countries, the NICs). When it comes to imposing trade restrictions, however, it is politically easier to attack the latter than the former, even though the former may be responsible for much more serious injury to domestic industry. The imposition of trade restrictions between member states is explicitly forbid-den by the Treaty of Rome and would therefore have immediate political consequences. Moreover, the member states conduct most of their foreign trade within the EEC, so that retaliation by the EEC acting as an entity or by the larger member states could hurt the exports of a recalcitrant member state much more than retaliation from individual third countries.

Consequently the protectionist urges are likely to manifest themselves *vis-à-vis* third countries first, although such protectionism could spill over and undermine the Common Market. If third country imports are barred by the weak EEC member states but retain free access to the strong members, and if free circulation within the EEC is maintained, the third country imports can easily find their way, via the strong member states (by changing the nationality of the products if necessary and possible), to the markets of the weak countries imposing the restrictions in the first place – this phenomenon is known as trade deflection. Because of the possibility of trade deflection, total free trade within the EEC is incompatible with different trade regimes *via-à-vis* the outside world. Thus, trade restrictions against third countries either will have to be imposed in common, or will lead to controls on trade between the member states, at first probably through devices such as strict controls on certificates of origin. These controls may be extended even to goods which are clearly labelled as being made in a member state. Eventually the Common Market may be undermined.

It is partly because of this link between protectionism against third countries and protectionism within the EEC that the Federal Republic of Germany has made free trade a matter of principle and has attempted to oppose dogmatically all protectionist measures by its EEC partners against whomever they might be directed. In theory, most trade matters *vis-à-vis* third countries belong *exclusively* to the domain of Community competence, so that the Federal Republic of Germany can veto in the Council any proposal to introduce restrictive measures. In practice, however, this blockage at the Community level could drive the member state seeking protectionist measures into going it alone and adopting unilateral measures, which might then spread to other member states. To prevent this happening, the Federal Republic would then have to make concessions in the Council. In both cases, the Germans would be faced with a dilemma. Either the principle of free trade is maintained rigidly, and the temptation for some of the others would be to cheat or to go it alone, thus threatening the CCP and the Common Market, or derogations of the principle are admitted by the Council, and protectionism is formally sanctioned

A few cases will now be examined to see how the divergence of perceived interests has influenced the determination of Community policies in this area.

Textiles

In 1977, on 23 June, France unilaterally introduced quantitative restrictions on French imports from third countries of four textile products (untreated cotton yarn; men's underwear; women's blouses and outer garments; and children's outer garments). The Commission regarded these as illegal and objected that such action should have been taken in a Community context. On 13 July it made proposals for measures which, roughly speaking, would have been less restrictive and more selective. These measures were regarded as providing Community covering for the French measures[1], though they were extended, for certain products and certain exporting countries, to other member states which had, once the French measures were known, also asked for a 'stabilization of the imports of sensitive products'.

Meanwhile international negotiations for the renewal of the Multi-Fibre Arrangement (MFA), which provides the framework for international trade in textiles and which brings together the developing countries, the EEC, the USA and Japan, began in Geneva (in July 1977). Probably with a view to influencing the outcome of these negotiations as well as to satisfying perceived French needs for protection, the French Government rejected the measures proposed by the Commission as 'unacceptable because insufficient'[2]. Noises were made to the effect that France had decided to go it alone if it did not obtain more restrictive dispositions concerning both the level of imports and the countries of origin.

The MFA negotiations were interrupted towards the end of July because agreement could not be reached between the EEC and the less-developed countries. On 12 August the Commission, bending to French pressures, announced further measures of import restrictions concerning: (1) trousers from Tunisia and Morocco into France; (2) men's shirts from Macao into France; (3) dresses and shirts from India to France, the United Kingdom and the Benelux countries; (4) sweaters and pullovers from Singapore into the United Kingdom and Ireland; (5) cotton cloth from Egypt into Italy and the United Kingdom and from Tunisia into the Benelux countries[3].

The EEC made its acceptance of the renewal of the MFA conditional upon the conclusion of satisfactory bilateral agreements between it and individual textile-exporting developing countries. These were pressured into concluding such bilateral agreements, and two days before the expiry of the existing MFA, on 29 December 1977, the EEC accepted the extension of the MFA for four years. Thus, the unilateral measures by France, supported by some of the other member states, succeeded in pushing EEC policy on textile imports towards a more protectionist stance.

Divergence and common policies

How could the divergent interests in textile imports of free-trading Germany and the Netherlands, on the one hand, and of protectionist France and Great Britain, on the other, be reconciled within the CCP? The answer was to depart from the principle of *uniformity* (Article 113 of the Treaty of

Rome says: '... the common commercial policy shall be based on uniform principles ...') and to retain the appearance of a common policy through procedures and formalities.

Within the overall import quotas for the EEC, there are individual national quotas for each of the member states. (These are not described as quotas, but as 'regional ceilings'.) This breakdown is applied for each year covered to each year covered to each product and to each exporting third country, so that the EEC textile quotas look as shown in *Table 6.1*.

Table 6.1 *EEC quantitative limits for certain textile products from third countries: cotton yarn*

Third countries	Member states[1]	Units	Quantitative limits from 1 January to 31 December[2]				
			1978	1979	1980	1981	1982
Argentina	D	Tonnes	1 116	1 118	1 120	1 122	1 124
	F		468	473	478	483	489
	I		424	425	427	429	431
	BNL		563	565	567	569	571
	UK		148	149	150	152	153
	IRL		53	55	57	59	61
	DK		67	68	69	70	71
	EEC		2 839	2 853	2 868	2 884	2 900
Brazil	D	Tonnes	11 740	11 758	11 776	11 794	11 812
	F		3 088	3 133	3 180	3 227	3 274
	I		3 364	3 378	3 391	3 405	3 419
	BNL		6 289	6 308	6 327	6 345	6 364
	UK		618	629	639	650	660
	IRL		1 350	1 369	1 390	1 410	1 431
	DK		451	459	467	475	482
	EEC		26 900	27 034	27 170	27 306	27 442
Colombia	D	Tonnes	3 510	3 515	3 520	3 524	3 529
	F		618	630	642	655	668
	I		946	950	953	957	961
	BNL		925	930	935	941	945
	UK		635	638	641	643	646
	IRL		300	305	311	316	322
	DK		275	277	279	281	283
	EEC		7 209	7 245	7 281	7 317	7 354
South Korea	D	Tonnes	304	305	306	307	307
	F		39	41	43	47	48
	I		14	15	15	16	17
	BNL		59	60	61	62	63
	UK		1	1	2	2	3
	IRL		—	1	2	3	4
	DK		1	1	2	2	2
	EEC		418	424	431	437	444

Hong Kong	D	Tonnes	14	14	15	15	16
	F		3	4	5	7	8
	I		27	27	28	28	28
	BNL		10	10	10	11	12
	UK		636	637	637	637	637
	IRL		18	20	20	20	21
	DK		2	2	2	3	3
	EEC		710	714	717	721	725
India	D	Tonnes	782	788	794	800	807
	F		511	526	542	557	573
	I		675	680	684	689	693
	BNL		717	723	730	736	742
	UK		5 941	5 944	5 948	5 952	5 955
	IRL		326	333	339	346	353
	DK		48	51	53	56	58
	EEC		9 000	9 045	9 090	9 136	9 181
Mexico	D	Tonnes	977	980	984	987	991
	F		721	721	730	739	748
	I		1 159	1 162	1 164	1 167	1 169
	BNL		2 074	2 077	2 081	2 084	2 088
	UK		84	86	88	90	92
	IRL		55	59	63	67	71
	DK		89	90	92	94	95
	EEC		5 150	5 175	5 202	5 228	5 254
Pakistan	D	Tonnes	1 466	1 470	1 476	1 480	1 485
	F		1 164	1 176	1 188	1 200	1 212
	I		1 963	1 967	1 970	1 974	1 977
	BNL		1 189	1 194	1 199	1 204	1 209
	UK		619	622	624	627	630
	IRL		381	386	391	397	402
	DK		218	220	222	224	226
	EEC		7 000	7 035	7 070	7 106	7 141
Peru	D	Tonnes	103	104	104	104	104
	F		2	3	3	5	6
	I		415	416	416	416	416
	BNL		—	—	1	1	1
	UK		—	—	1	1	1
	IRL		—	—	1	1	2
	DK		10	10	10	10	11
	EEC		530	533	536	538	541
Romania	D	Tonnes	990	993	996	998	1 001
	F		363	370	378	385	393
	I		10	12	14	17	19
	BNL		16	19	22	25	28
	UK		15	17	18	20	22
	IRL		18	21	24	28	31
	DK		11	12	14	15	16
	EEC		1 423	1 444	1 466	1 488	1 510

Table 6.1 – contd

Third countries	Member states[1]	Units	Quantitative limits from 1 January to 31 December[2]				
			1978	1979	1980	1981	1982
Yugoslavia	D	Tonnes	2 747	2 752	2 757	2 762	2 767
	F		150	163	176	188	201
	I		4 289	4 293	4 297	4 300	4 304
	BNL		98	103	108	114	119
	UK		123	126	129	132	135
	IRL		27	32	38	44	49
	DK		23	25	27	29	32
	EEC		7 457	7 494	7 532	7 569	7 607

1. D = Federal Republic of Germany   BNL= Belgium, Netherlands and Luxembourg
   F = France   IRL = Ireland
   I = Italy   DK = Denmark
2. According to Council Regulation (EEC) No. 1176/79, 'the breakdown between Member
   States of the Community quantitative limits shall be definitive for the years 1978 and 1979.
   For the years 1980 to 1982, this breakdown is published for the purposes of information and
   its definitive version shall be the subject of a Community Regulation at the beginning of each
   of those years.'
Source: EEC Regulation 1176/79 of 12 June 1979, published in the *Official Journal of the
   European Communities*, 18 June 1979, No. L149.

The breakdown shown in *Table 6.1* for one single product (cotton yarn
not put up for retail sale) was repeated for another 122 product categories in
EEC Regulation 1176/79, resulting in a very long schedule indeed. From the
point of view of the third-country exporters, what matters is the quantitative
limits, not of the EEC as a whole, but of individual member states.

Textiles are a good example of the *differentiated* application of a common
policy, which allows each member state to do more or less what it wants
within a Community context. Another important and striking example
concerns the *legal* right conferred on member states, under certain conditions, unilaterally to adopt surveillance and/or protective measures against
imports. According to Council Regulation (EEC) No. 926/79 of 8 May 1979
on common rules for imports[4]:

'... Whereas the common commercial policy must be based on uniform
principles; ... Whereas Member States should be empowered, in certain
circumstances and provided that their actions are on an interim basis only,
to take protective measures individually: ...

'*Article 9*
'2. In cases of extreme urgency the Member State may carry out
surveillance at national level after informing the Commission according
with Article 3. ...

'*Article 14*

'2 (b) Where a Member State claims that the matter is especially urgent, consultations shall take place within a period of five working days following information transmitted to the Commission: at the end of this period, the Member State may take these [protective] measures. ...

'4 ... The measures shall operate only until the coming into operation of the decision taken by the Commission. However, where the Commission decides not to introduce any measure or adopts measures ... different from those taken by the Member State, its decision shall apply as from the sixth day following its entry into force, unless the Member State which has taken the measures refers the decision to the Council; in that case, the national measures shall continue to operate until the entry into force of the decision taken by the Council, but in no case beyond the expiry of a period of one month following referral of the matter to the latter. The Council shall take a decision before the expiry of that period. ...'

These words and sentences give a good idea of the flavour of Community business. Roughly speaking, what is being said seems to be that, provided certain procedures and formalities concerning consultation and information are observed, a Member State may legally take unilateral measures of import surveillance and/or restrictions, but that the latter have to be approved by the Commission or the Council or else they will lapse after roughly one month. Yet the textile example given earlier shows that it is very difficult to undo a *fait accompli* and that a member state is not likely to rescind the unilateral measures it has adopted unless it obtains some concessions. In any case, the European Court of Justice does not dispose of independent powers of enforcement against national governments.

Since such conflicts are difficult to resolve, Regulation 926/79, like many other Community legal instruments, confines itself to laying down procedures and formalities. Procedure has therefore assumed an increasing burden in Community business, as a substitute for the resolution of the substance of divergences and conflicts.

Steel

In 1977 there was a significant deterioration in the situation of the steel industry in the EEC: capacity utilization fell to 60 per cent for the EEC as a whole, and exports fell by 27 per cent and imports rose by 67 per cent compared with the last good year, 1974[5].

On 17 November 1977, a communiqué by Eurofer, the EEC steel producers' club, called for protectionist measures. A week later, the French Minister for Industry, M. René Monory, declared that France would take 'its responsibilities' (meaning national measures) if new EEC measures did not enter into force by 1 January[6]. On 2 December Sir Charles Villiers, Chairman of the British Steel Corporation, called for action by Brussels[7]. On 17 December 1977, the *Guardian* reported that, because the Federal Republic of Germany had dogmatically prevented the adoption of earlier proposals by the Commission, the British and French Governments were ready to go it alone and adopt national measures to restrict imports. Then the Germans gave in, an additional factor being the poor condition of their own steel industry. Around 20 December, the Nine agreed on a comprehensive system of minimum prices for a number of steel products, and on an immediate application of anti-dumping duties on imports of these products, the duties being defined as the difference between the import prices and the minimum prices. The anti-dumping duties were to be applied for an initial period of three months, during which time voluntary agreements were to be negotiated with major third countries on the quantities and the prices of their steel exports to the EEC.

The Davignon Plan, as it came to be called, was fairly successful in controlling imports and maintaining prices. It was, however, much less successful in guiding a restructuring of the industry on a rational European basis: restructuring was undertaken on an individual, national basis. Also, its system of voluntary production quotas did not stand up to the pressures of a deepening recession: faced with falling prices and the reluctance of the German and Italian industries to accept voluntary cuts in production levels, the Council of the European Communities declared, on 30 October 1980, a state of 'manifest crisis' in the steel sector[8], which, under Article 58 of the European Coal and Steel Community Treaty, gave the Commission powers to establish and enforce mandatory production quotas.

One explanation for these different degrees of success is that agreement between member states and their steel industries depends on a convergence of interests, and that such a convergence is easier to secure when all Nine stand to gain, if necessary at the expense of outsiders (through import restrictions). Divergence of perceived interests may prevail, however, when there is no more to be gained from third countries and when it becomes a question of allocating reductions in member states' capacities (through restructuring) and output levels (through production on quotas and cuts). Agreement is then much more difficult to secure.

Summary and conclusions

The fear that economic divergence between the strong and the weak may combine with the world recession to provoke unilateral protectionist measures by the weaker member states, thus undermining the Common Market, is a very real one. The dilemma facing the Community and the strong countries is that a rigid insistence on free trade may increase the temptation to the weak to cheat or to adopt unilateral measures, thus undermining the Common Market, while concessions, derogations and the adoption of protectionist measures at the Community level also risk undermining the Common Market. One apparent way of dealing with this problem is to differentiate the applications of the Common Commercial Policy, as with the regional ceilings for textiles or the legal possibility for a member state to adopt national measures of trade surveillance or restrictions, although the policy then risks becoming uncommon in all but name and procedure, thus again threatening to undermine the Common Market.

The case of steel illustrates that it is easier to secure a convergence of interests when everyone stands to gain (if necessary, at the expense of outsiders) than when cuts in output and capacity have to be allocated between member states.

1 *Le Monde*, 9 July 1977.
2 *Le Monde*, 15 July 1977.
3 *Le Monde*, 14–15 August 1977.
4 *Official Journal of the European Communities*, 29 May 1979.
5 See The International Monetary Fund, *The Rise in Protectionism*, Washington DC, 1978.
6 *Le Monde*, 25 November 1977.
7 *The Times*, 3 December 1977.
8 See the article by P. Lemaître in 'Europa', *The Times*, 3 February 1981.

Bibliographical note

Strangely enough (or perhaps it is not so strange, in view of the sensitiveness of the issues involved), there have been very few empirical studies of how the CCP works in practice. On industrial adjustment and protectionism in steel, textiles and shipbuilding, see: S. Strange, 'The management of surplus capacity: or how does theory stand up to protectionism 1970s style?', *International Organisation*, Summer 1979; S. Woolcock, 'Industrial adjustment: the Community dimension', in: M. Hodges and W. Wallace (eds.), *Economic Divergence in the EC*, London, Allen & Unwin, 1981; L. Tsoukalis and A. da Silva Ferreira, 'Management of industrial surplus capacity in the EC', *International Organisation*, Summer 1980.

Community Energy Policy[1]

In the previous two chapters I have argued that the crucial link between the divergence of economic developments and the emergence of political problems in the Community is the divergence of perceived interests between member states. Developments in the energy field show that divergences of perceived interests can arise independently of any divergence in inflation rates, growth rates, income levels, etc. The convergence and divergence of perceived national interests, changing as they have done over time, have been major determinants of the development of Community energy policy. Convergence of perceived interests has made it possible to achieve convergence of national policies and progress in implementing common policies. Conversely, while the failure of common policies has often been laid at the door of divergent national policies (sometimes meaning different styles of national policy), of different energy-resource endowments, or of different degrees of dependence on imported energy, it is hard to see why these factors should, by themselves, discourage co-operation between EEC member states (after all, differences in resource endowments should be conducive to trade) were it not for the existence of divergent perceptions of national interests.

Coal

The European Coal and Steel Community (ECSC) was established by the Treaty of Paris in 1951 (see the appendix to this chapter for details). Its creation depended on a convergence of national interests. After the Second World War, the control of the coal industry in West Germany lay with the Allies in the International Ruhr Authority. By 1950, however, the East –West conflict, the American insistence that West Germany should become a full member of the Western alliance, and the extent of German economic recovery combined to make this direct foreign control of an important part of the German economy increasingly untenable. France became fearful lest her traditional enemy regained full national control of the two heavy industries, which were then considered to be the basis of military and economic power. Under the inspiration of Jean Monnet, Robert Schuman, the French Foreign Minister, proposed the pooling of German and French coal and steel resources in a complex arrangement with supranational features that were meant to make war between the two countries impossible. The other Western European countries were then invited to join, and the Americans supported the venture. (The United Kingdom refused to join.)

An important lesson from this achievement is that it sometimes requires an act of statesmanship and vision to bring about a convergence of perceived national interests, for interests are neither given immutably nor independent of human perceptions, human arrangements and human endeavours. The genius and greatness of Jean Monnet and Robert Schuman was that they transformed a situation of historical hostility into one of common interest.

During the 1950s, the ECSC benefited from a convergence of national interests: the desire of France, the Benelux countries and, to some extent, Italy, to obtain secure and non-discriminatory access to coal from West Germany, the largest producing country on the continent outside the Iron Curtain, and the desire of West Germany itself to regain its sovereignty and to be recognized as a full member of the international system[2]. During the 1950s, this convergence of national interests was made much easier by the combination of rising demand for, and production of, coal. The ECSC was seen to benefit both the exporting and the importing member states. It seems much easier for nations to agree on the distribution of benefits in an environment of growth than to agree on the distribution of costs at a time of recession and/or contraction[3].

It is sometimes argued that the major factor inhibiting European integration or the development of a common policy in any sector is the lack of policy instruments at the level of the Community; in other words, just as the Community now has its 'own financial resources', so it needs to have its 'own policy instruments'. There is, however, a vital difference between the legal existence of certain powers and instruments, and the ability actually to use them. Under the Treaty of Paris (Article 58), the High Authority disposes of considerable powers of intervention in the event of a *'manifest crisis'* being declared. Such a crisis did indeed develop in 1958–60, from a combination of falling demand for energy as a whole and rising imports of oil and coal. Stocks of coal at the pithead in ECSC countries rose from 7.3 million tonnes in 1957 to 24.7 million tonnes in 1958 and 31.2 million tonnes in 1959[3]. Despite repeated attempts by the High Authority, which proposed to introduce production quotas and import restrictions, a state of manifest crisis could not be declared because the Council withheld its consent. In the May 1959 vote, the Benelux countries supported the High Authority, but France, Germany and Italy opposed it. The French and Italian position can be understood with reference to their interest in cheap, imported sources of energy, but why did Germany, with its important coal industry, oppose the High Authority? In fact Germany, like France, was reluctant to transfer important powers to the supranational level.

In 1958, first Belgium, then the Federal Republic took national measures to limit coal imports from third countries. France had already done so. It remained for the High Authority to 'approve' these measures and to 'harmonize' them in a Community framework. From the end of the 1950s onwards, the advent of abundant and cheap Middle Eastern oil changed the energy situation dramatically. In the Europe of Nine, coal output fell from 436.9 million tonnes in 1960 to 270.2 million tonnes in 1973, and its share of total energy consumption fell from around 75 per cent in 1950 to 21 per cent in 1973. The nature of the problems facing policy-makers in the coal subsector changed; it was now a question, in coal-producing countries, of easing the process of contraction. Again, the ECSC could not agree on a real common policy, because of the divergence in perceived interests between Germany, with its important coal-mining industry, and France and Italy, which were poor in indigenous resources and which did not want to pay more for their coal to subsidize Germany. The Community system of state aids involves no Community protection (through quotas and tariffs) and no Community financing; it simply means that the national aids are 'authorized' by the High Authority according to Community rules which give the system an appearance of a common policy. (For coking coal, however, a system of Community subsidies for intra-Community trade in coking coal and coke produced in the Community was instituted in 1966, whereby the burden was shared forty/sixty between the producing country and a Community common fund.)

Since the 1973–4 oil crisis, the Community has formally adopted a set of Energy Policy Objectives for 1985[4] (by the Council Resolution of 17 December 1974) which envisage, *inter alia*, arresting the decline of coal and maintaining Community production at the level of 250 million tonnes. The means potentially available at the Community level for achieving this include: (a) Community subsidies on the production or stockpiling of coal; (b) Community subsidies to encourage the burning of coal in Community power stations and to finance the conversion of power stations from oil-burning to coal-burning; and (c) Community subsidies on intra-Community trade in coal. In 1977 and 1978, the Council was twice unable to agree to Commission proposals in these directions, mainly because of divergences of interests between the member states. The proposals would have benefited mainly the United Kingdom (the largest Community producer) and the Federal Republic of Germany (the second largest), but the United Kingdom with an avowed anti-European Energy Minister (Mr Benn) under the last Labour Government, apparently offered nothing in return and would not make any concessions in the energy field (and in many other fields too) to induce the other countries to accept the costs involved. For these countries, there is always the option of importing cheaper coal from Poland, South Africa, the USA, etc. In 1978, for example, extra-Community imports of coal represented 16 per cent of coal consumption in the Community. Moreover, British coal was not only more costly, but, because of strikes, was not considered on the continent as a secure source of supply.

Despite the Community's objectives for 1985, Community coal ouput has continued to decline, year by year, since 1973 under the impetus of rising costs, depressed demand (especially from the steel sector, which is in a state of crisis) and competition from other fuels and imported coal: from 270.2 million tonnes in 1973 it has fallen to 238.1 million tonnes in 1978 and 237.4 million tonnes in 1979. Thus although the ECSC attempts to maintain equitable conditions of competition in the coal market, there is still no common energy policy in coal in the sense of a genuine Community solidarity and a common approach to encouraging Community coal production and utilization.

Nuclear energy

The treaty establishing the European Atomic Energy Community (Euratom) was signed in Rome in March 1957, at the same time as the treaty establishing the European Economic Community (EEC). Euratom was created to develop the civilian use of nuclear energy at a time when the Suez Canal crisis (1956) had cast doubts on the reliability of Middle Eastern oil (for details, see the appendix to this chapter).

The creation of Euratom shows how a convergence of interests can be engineered through the technique of linkage. In 1956, the French were very enthusiastic about the idea of Euratom and saw it as a support for their military nuclear programme; they were, however, much less interested in the idea of the Common Market than the Germans and the Benelux, and less interested in the free circulation of workers and the European Investment Bank than the Italians. Fearing that the French Parliament would only ratify the Euratom treaty, the Five insisted on the link between the two treaties, which were signed on the same day.

Compared with its ambitious goals, Euratom was a failure. Part of the reason was that nuclear energy lost much of its urgency with the changed international energy situation, the Suez crisis being followed by the renewal of abundant oil supplies from the Middle East. Another major reason was the divergence of interests and strategies of the member states. The initial convergence of perceived interests was based partly on a number of French expectations[3] which were probably unrealistic and which could not be satisfied in the event, and while the German Government had supported Euratom for political reasons (in order to get France to accept the Common Market), this support did not trickle down to the level of German industry. From the beginning there was little sharing of information, research or investment by France and Germany. With its considerable advance at the research level, France pressed ahead with its national military and civilian programme, and exploited the escape clause in the treaty which suspended the obligation to share information if defence interests were involved. German industrialists, with their powerful industrial base and weakness in basic research, preferred to co-operate with the large American firms (General Electric, Westinghouse). This divergence of interests was reflected in the dispute over whether Euratom should develop the natural-uranium system (French) or the enriched-uranium system (American). Despite the existence of four establishments under the Common Research Centre, at Ispra (Italy), Geel (Belgium), Petten (Netherlands), and Karlsruhe (Germany), the activities of the Common Research were marginalized, as the member states entrusted the most promising researches to their own, national laboratories.

Although the French eventually abandoned the natural-uranium system around 1970 and went for the enriched-uranium, light-water systems developed by the Americans, there is still no integrated Community reactor construction industry. In the enrichment of uranium, however, there are two European groups: Eurodif led by France (and which groups together France, Italy, Belgium and Spain) and using the gaseous diffusion technique, and Urenco, grouping together the United Kingdom, Federal Republic of Germany and the Netherlands, and using the centrifuge technique. Both groups are outside the legal framework of the European Communities, and neither has the status of a 'joint undertaking' under the Euratom treaty. In the development of the next generation of 'fast breeders', France, the United Kingdom and the Federal Republic of Germany are in competition with each other, but the electricity boards of Germany, France and Italy have a co-operative agreement to build in common the first few large-scale plants. Looking still further ahead, to the concept of nuclear *fusion* (the phenomenon occurring in a hydrogen-bomb explosion and in the sun), after years of hard bargaining between member states, an agreement was reached in October 1977 to site an experimental prototype, the Joint European Torus (JET), at Culham in England. JET is a joint undertaking under the Euratom Treaty, and is financed to the extent of 80 per cent by the Community (148 million units of account for the period 1976–80), 10 per cent by the United Kingdom and 10 per cent by the other participants, including Sweden and Switzerland. It thus appears easier to get agreement on something for which the application is far off than on a technology whose industrial application is near at hand.

Because of environmental and safety concerns, the nuclear energy programmes have been slowed down or indefinitely postponed in all countries in the European Communities with the sole exception of France. For 1985, the expected contribution of nuclear energy is less than half of the level (200 gigawatts, amounting to 17 per cent of total Community energy consumption) envisaged in the December 1974 Resolution. It is clear that this shortcoming cannot be laid at the Community's door; the obstacles lie in each of the countries, and even a real federation like the USA is having similar problems.

Petroleum

It is in the area of oil policies that the divergences of interests between member states have been so marked that the question arises as to whether the European Community deserves to be called a community at all.

During the 1973–4 oil crisis, the Netherlands was specifically subjected to an Arab embargo because of its professed sympathies for Isreal. The European Community was not able, at least publicly, to manifest its solidarity with the Dutch, for fear of Arab reprisals, and France and the United Kingdom adopted what was seen as a *sauve-qui-peut* attitude and sought bilateral deals with individual Arab states. Whatever sharing of oil supplies did in fact take place was implemented by the oil majors (the large multinational oil companies).

Although there is a Council Directive since 1968 (Directive 68/414/EEC) requiring member states to maintain sixty-five days of oil stocks, which were subsequently increased to ninety days (Directive 72/425/EEC), and although Article 34 of the EEC Treaty clearly states that 'Quantitative restrictions on exports, and all measures having equivalent effect, shall be prohibited between Member States', the European Communities do not have a semi-automatic oil-sharing scheme comparable to that of the International Energy Agency (IEA), which includes most OECD countries with the notable exception of France, and which was set up in November 1974 under United States leadership. Under the IEA agreement, in the event of a shortfall in supplies of 7 per cent affecting any or all participating countries, the oil-sharing scheme would be automatically activated unless members decided otherwise by a special majority. The most that the European Community has been able to agree on, to date, is contained in the Council Decision of 7 November 1977, adopted after many wranglings:

> 'Where difficulties arise in the supply of crude oil or petrolum products in one or more Member States, the Commission ... may set a target for reducing consumption ... up to 10 per cent of normal consumption. ... The quantities of petroleum products saved ... shall be shared out between the Member States. ...'

Thus, not only are the provisions vaguer than in the IEA agreement, but there is no automaticity: the Commission may propose, but the Council does not have to agree. As between national policies and international co-operation at the OECD level, the European Community risks losing its relevance and specificity.

One reason for this mixed success is that it is often easier to achieve a convergence of interests and a consensus between a number of nation states when there is a recognized and undisputed leader, a hegemonic power enjoying a great superiority in means and power. The unification of Europe may be an unprecedentedly difficult venture because, unlike for example the *Zollverein* in the nineteenth century, which contained a dominant power (Prussia), it is an attempt to integrate equals.

Divergence of perceived national interests, of interests often defined in a narrow-minded, short-term manner, frequently underlay developments in Community policy concerning oil. One way of encouraging more oil prospecting is to set a minimum support price (MSP). While the IEA was able to agree to an MSP in 1976, within the EEC the subject has caused bitter arguments between the United Kingdom and France, which feared that it might have to subsidize North Sea oil. Agreement was never reached, and the United Kingdom eventually dropped the proposal. Although in the context of rising oil prices an MSP at the levels originally envisaged (US$7 per barrel) became increasingly irrelevant, the disputes nevertheless succeeded in creating a great deal of ill-feeling in the EEC.

As the economic recession spread, excess capacity began to develop in oil refineries in the EEC. The rate of capacity utilization, which had been 85 per cent in 1963–73, fell to 58 per cent in 1975, 62 per cent in 1976, and 63 per cent in 1977[5]. In March 1977, the Commission proposed a reduction of capacity and a temporary suspension of national aids to the construction of new refineries. Agreement was blocked by the United Kingdom, which was opposed to any interference with the planned expansion of UK refining capacity in respect of North Sea oil. It is arguable whether such a policy was in the best interests of the United Kingdom: a refinery brings few jobs, and the value added can be rather low and has to be weighed against the loss of the price premium that North Sea crude commands because of its being of a light quality. The position taken by the United Kingdom led not surprisingly, to retaliation by Italy and France, which vetoed the Commission's proposals for subsidizing Community coal (see above). The United Kingdom also rejected suggestions that it should maintain normal supply flows in times of crisis.

It is not hard to see in broad terms how a powerful convergence of interests can be engineered here[6]. The United Kingdom's EEC partners are very interested in access to North Sea oil, which they see as a potential lifebuoy in times of crisis, and suggestions that they are out to beat the United Kingdom into selling at prices below market levels do not seem justified. The United Kingdom, for its part, needs an improvement in its relations with its EEC partners, a radical reform of the CAP and of the Community's budgetary rules, and perhaps also Community assistance in regenerating its industrial base and in exploiting its coal and other energy resources. Unfortunately, leaders of the calibre of Jean Monnet, Robert Schuman and Konrad Adenauer do not seem to be coming forward to bring such a convergence of interests about. There is also a serious problem of traditional British perceptions. Until now, the Conservative Government of Mrs Thatcher, like its Labour predecessor,

> 'has taken the view that the exploitation of the British sector of the North Sea is Britain's business and nobody else's. It has rejected any suggestion that the other members of the Community should get preferential access to, or preferential prices for, oil from the North Sea, on the grounds that Community countries are already, through normal market forces, receiving about half of Britain's gross exports of North Sea oil, and that on the price front Britain is necessarily only a follower, not a leader, of the market. *A fortiori*, it consistently rejected arguments from Community countries that there was or should be a link between the North Sea and the renegotiation of the rules governing Britain's contribution to the Community budget'[6].

What British Governments may have failed to appreciate is that such arguments, however correct in themselves, may be taken by the United Kingdom's partners in the EEC to mean: 'We, the fortunate British, refuse to come to the assistance of our friends in times of need.'

Between 1973 and 1978, while EEC net oil imports declined from more than 500 million tonnes of oil equivalent (toe) to 472 million toe, under the impact of both reduced consumption and increased North Sea production, net oil imports by the USA increased by 42.5 per cent, from 287 million toe to 409 million toe. The impact on the oil market and on the value of the dollar has been highly negative. At the Tokyo summit of the seven major Western countries at the end of June 1979, the USA, Japan and the EEC agreed to limit their oil imports for 1985 to given quantitative targets. The question arose of dividing the overall ceiling for the EEC between individual member states. This must have been a most difficult negotiating task, but the need to make the USA stick to its part of the agreement forced the EEC countries to reach agreement by the end of September 1979. They were helped in this by the prospect that the United Kingdom imports would soon become negative (the United Kingdom would become a small net exporter), which would allow other countries to import more within the overall ceiling.

Finally, the fact that, in times of short supplies, prices on the Rotterdam free market tend to shoot up to a much higher level than OPEC contractual prices has been blamed as a factor encouraging or enabling general price rises, the argument being that OPEC producers use these prices to justify raising their contractual prices. France has been leading a move to make the Rotterdam market more 'transparent' in an effort to stabilize prices. The Federal Republic and the United Kingdom have, however, been less than enthusiastic, the former because its economic strength and the value of the

Deutschmark enable it to buy its way out of trouble and because it relies to a large extent on the Rotterdam market, the United Kingdom because it hosts a number of oil majors and does not like controls.

Summary and conclusions

The convergence and divergence of perceived interests have played a major role in shaping the evolution of Community energy policies. The creation of the ECSC was due in no small part to the genius and vision of people like Robert Schuman and Jean Monnet in engineering a convergence of interests between hereditary foes. The early stages of the ECSC benefited from a convergence of interests brought about by rising demand for and rising production of coal, but the crisis of 1958–60 brought this to an end and showed that divergence of perceived interests could paralyse common action, despite the legal existence of Community policy instruments. Since the 1973–4 oil crisis, the failure to implement a Community policy to encourage coal production is again attributable to the divergence of perceived national interests.

The creation of Euratom showed how a convergence of interests could be brought about through the technique of linkage, but its subsequent history belied initial hopes, mainly because the initial convergence was replaced by a divergence of interests between France and Germany. It was, however, possible to get agreement on the JET project, partly because it was far removed from the application phase.

Divergences of perceived interests have been most marked and bitter in the case of petroleum. This is not surprising, since so much is at stake, petroleum representing the largest source of energy for the West. The case of North Sea oil suggests, on the one hand, that entrenched attitudes and perceptions may be more important than material circumstances in shaping policy. On the other hand, the need to speak with one voice, in order, for example, to make the USA abide by oil import targets, has made for a convergence of interests.

There appears to be little chance of a common energy policy on the lines of the CAP. It is now a question of achieving a convergence of national policies; this presupposes a convergence of perceived interests, but this convergence requires statesmanship and vision to bring it about.

Failure to achieve this may have consequences of the utmost gravity. As the 'Three Wise Men' report[7] suggested, a great danger in the future may be 'the competition among Member States to guarantee themselves supplies of oil or natural gas which will allow them to maintain the maximum level of economic activity. This danger would be particularly great in the case of disturbance in one or another oil-producing country, which could bring a fresh interruption in supplies for a longer or shorter period.'

The European Coal and Steel Community and Euratom

The European Coal and Steel Community (ECSC), established by the Treaty of Paris in April 1951, is the oldest of the three European Communities. It is also the most supranational in inspiration, vesting the High Authority (now the Commission) with considerable powers of intervention. As stated in the Treaty, the aims of ECSC are to ensure, within a common market for coal and steel: orderly supply; equal access for consumers; low prices; the removal of intra-Community import and export duties, quantitative restrictions, state aids and subsidies, and restrictive practices; to promote modernization and expansion; and to promote improved working conditions and living standards for the workers. The High Authority is empowered: to obtain the information it requires; to impose fines on firms evading their obligations; to raise revenue by imposing levies (normally not to exceed 1 per cent) on the production of coal and steel; to contract loans for the purposes of financing or guaranteeing investments; and finally to impose production quotas and other necessary measures in the event of a *manifest* crisis. The consent of the Council is necessary only in certain important matters, and unanimity is required in even fewer instances. These supranational powers reflected the mood of the time. Thus, whereas under the Treaties of Rome (EEC and Euratom) the Council decides on the Commission's proposal, under the Treaty of Paris the Commission decides with the Council's endorsement.

The Euratom treaty was very ambitious and provided for:

The co-ordination of research and investments, the latter to be notified obligatorily to the Commission.

Pluri-annual common research programmes to be executed by a Common Research Centre.

A common system for the dissemination of information.

A common supply policy for ores, source materials and special fissile materials, on the principle of equal access for Community users. The Supply Agency was to have a right of option on all fuels produced in the Community and an exclusive right to conclude contracts relating to the supply of fuels coming from inside or outside the Community.

A status of 'joint undertaking' to facilitate inter-country industrial co-operation.

'Association contracts' which would allow the Community to participate financially in research undertaken by member states and to diffuse the results.

Regarding the Supply Agency, the Commission had for a long time contented itself simply with authorizing, retrospectively, the contracts signed by the member states, but in November 1978, at the demand of Belgium in connection with an International Atomic Energy Agency (IAEA) conference in Vienna on the 'physical protection of fissile materials', the European Court of Justice reaffirmed the competence of Euratom. This provoked a furore in France, which, in September 1979, asked for a modification of Chapter 6 of the treaty dealing with supplies. The French argument is that there cannot be the same free circulation of dangerous materials (e.g. plutonium) as of potatoes, unless there is a common position on non-proliferation.

1 For a more comprehensive treatment, see Y.S. Hu, 'Energy policy', in: Ali El-Agraa (ed.), *The Economics of the European Community*, Oxford, Philip Allan, 1980.
2 Ulf Lantzke, Director-General of the IEA, 'International cooperation on energy', *The World Today*, March 1976.
3 N. J. D. Lucas, *Energy and the European Communities*, London, 1977.
4 The main aim was to reduce dependence on imported energy, which stood at 61 per cent in 1973, to about 50 per cent in 1985. The overall pattern of demand for primary energy in 1985 would then look as follows, as compared with the earlier forecasts: solid fuels, 17 per cent instead of 10; oil, 47 per cent instead of 64; natural gas, 20 per cent instead of 15; hydroelectric and geothermal energy, 3 per cent instead of 2; nuclear energy, 13 per cent instead of 9.

The resolution did not indicate the breakdown of the targets between the individual member states; nor did it specify by what means, and at what stages, the targets were to be attained. The targets, therefore, amount to little more than a general declaration of intent, with little operational significance.
5 Michel Bacchetta, 'Oil refining in the European Community', *Journal of Common Market Studies*, December 1978.
6 R. Dafter and I. Davidson, *North Sea Oil and Gas and British Foreign Policy*, London, Royal Institute of International Affairs, 1980.
7 Committee of Three to the European Council, *Report on European Institutions*, Brussels, October 1979.

Bibliographical note

Although there are many technical studies of energy problems and individual fuels (dealing for example with long-term supply and demand projections or the optimal rate of depletion), there are very few works on actual energy policies in EEC countries. The best book is that by N. J. D. Lucas, op. cit. See also Guy de Carmoy, *Energy for Europe, Economic and Political Implications*, Washington DC, American Enterprise Institute for Public Policy Research, 1977; and Commission of the European Communities, *Community Energy Policy: Texts of the Relevant Legislation*, Brussels, 1976, 1979. On British North Sea oil and the EEC, see R. Dafter and I. Davidson, op. cit., and M. Shackleton, 'Oil and the British foreign policy process', *Millennium*, Autumn 1978.

The European Monetary System

It is often argued either (by the French and Germans) that the success of the European Monetary System (EMS) depends on a convergence of inflation rates or (by the sceptical British and Americans) that the EMS will not work because there is too much difference in the inflation rates of the participants. This chapter adopts an unorthodox view[1] and argues that the EMS has to be seen in a wider context than simply that of its exchange-rate mechanism; whether the EMS will be a success or failure, and the way in which it will probably evolve, depend on what the wider objectives of the EMS are. Moreover, even at a mechanical level, it is not at all self-evident that divergent inflation rates are necessarily incompatible with a fair degree of exchange-rate stability, as I will attempt to show. The mechanisms of the EMS are described in an appendix to this chapter.

Convergence of interests in relation to the dollar

The EMS is built on a convergence of interests *vis-à-vis* what is called the dollar problem and results from years of increasing European dissatisfaction with the system (or nonsystem) that followed the breakdown of the Bretton Woods system in the early 1970s.

The Bretton Woods system enshrined the US dollar's role as the world's international money or parallel currency. The dollar has been widely used: as a reserve asset by central banks; as a means of settlement between central banks and other agents; as a currency for market interventions by central banks; to denominate most international contracts; as the *numéraire* against which the exchange rates of other countries were defined, stabilized, devalued or revalued; as the currency in which private firms and individuals kept the bulk of their working balances for international purposes; and so on.

In return for the power, influence, and freedom from balance-of-payments constraints that all this conferred on the USA, financial orthodoxy as well as international fair play required that the USA should assume its responsibilities for the dollar. These responsibilities included the maintenance of the dollar's value (broadly defined) and of its convertibility (again broadly defined).

Although General de Gaulle disliked the power and influence which the role of the dollar gave the USA, what drove the Federal Republic of Germany and the Europeans to undertake the EMS was not dissatisfaction with the Bretton Woods system, but exasperation with the inconvertible *paper-dollar* standard that took its place in 1971, when President Nixon suspended the automatic convertibility of the dollar into gold (and other currencies) at a fixed rate, and with the resulting system of floating exchange rates. This situation has entailed what are perceived as serious economic, financial, and commercial losses for the Europeans. First, the flooding of the international monetary system by a creation of dollars that was not subject to the usual balance-of-payments constraints is widely perceived as having been a major cause of the considerable rise in inflation rates world-wide. Secondly, the depreciation of the dollar has entailed huge losses for all those holding dollars, including central banks which have had to purchase massive amounts of dollars in order to slow the rate of appreciation of their currencies. The book-keeping losses reported by the Deutsche Bundesbank amounted to DM43 000 million for the period 1971–8, more than three times the total international reserves of the Federal Republic at the end of 1969, and about half the value of its reserves on average in 1978. Thirdly, it is feared that the depreciation of the dollar, by making US exports more competitive, could have serious consequences for European industries competing at home and abroad with US exports.

In European eyes, there is no sign of an early improvement in the situation. The astronomical amount of dollars in circulation in the world, known as the dollar 'overhang', a phenomenon which has been exacerbated by the functioning of the Eurodollar market, means that even a very small percentage switch by dollar holders into other currencies can have a very large unsettling impact on the value of the dollar. These portfolio adjustments may be triggered by politico-military developments (in connection, for example, with US policy in the Middle East) as well as by lack of confidence in the ability of the US Government 'to keep its house in order'. Apart from the dollar overhang, other grounds for pessimism concerning the dollar problem include doubts about the quality of US leadership, trends in US imports of petroleum, and the lack of progress in reforming the international monetary system.

Thus, in the words of Professor Robert Triffin, a leading observer of international monetary problems who predicted the breakdown of the Bretton Woods system a decade before it happened[2]:

'The Bremen initiative [on the EMS] ... reflects, at bottom, a desperate desire of the leaders of the Community to make their countries less dependent on the unpredictable vagaries of a shrinking USA dollar.'

How was this dependence on and vulnerability to the dollar to be reduced? It was to be done by reducing the Europeans' use of the dollar as a reserve asset, a means of settlement, a currency of market intervention, a currency in which international contracts are denominated, a currency in which private working balances are kept, and the currency against which exchange rates are defined, stabilized, revalued and devalued. This presupposes, of course, the existence of a suitable alternative whose use can be promoted for the aforementioned purposes, an alternative under the control of the Europeans, an alternative which pools the strength of the individual European currencies in order to make it equal to its task.

If, therefore, the principal motivation for the EMS is the Europeans' dissatisfaction with the paper-dollar standard, it follows that the central piece of the EMS, the criterion by whch it will be judged a success or failure, is the European Currency Unit (ECU) and its future institutional underpinning, the European Monetary Fund (EMF) (for details see the appendix to this chapter). The modalities of the use of the ECU and the shape of the EMF have not yet been decided definitively, but the system is flexible and is capable of evolution. It should also be noted that the ECU may well displace the dollar in international uses rather than or before domestic European currencies in domestic uses. The existence of the ECU and the EMF may also provide a basis for increased European weight and bargaining power in the international monetary arena, which can only mean a diminution in the dollar's hegemony. This is certainly one of the major reasons why the USA and its traditional ally, the United Kingdom, view the EMS initiative with some apprehension and display an ambivalent attitude towards it.

Divergent inflation rates and exchange rate stability

In comparison with the grand design behind the ECU and the EMF, the question of exchange rates between the participating currencies assumes a secondary importance. Exchange rate stability is a means to an end. It is important to the extent that it is necessary for the promotion of the international use of the ECU. This means that the EMS may turn out to be a success even if several exchange rate adjustments take place, provided that these do not irretrievably undermine the credibility of the ECU. (It is difficult to be certain about this, because the EMS represents a novel experiment in the annals of international monetary history and there is not much previous experience that one can refer to.) The credibility of the ECU, however, may depend much more on political factors (in the USA, Europe and the rest of the world) and wider economic and financial considerations than simply exchange rates between EMS currencies.

Moreover, at a technical level, it is not true that divergence of inflation rates is necessarily incompatible with exchange rate stability. The argument here is based on the fact or assumption that a currency's exchange rate is determined, in the long or medium term, by its relative purchasing power, so that relative exchange rate movements are determined, over the same period, by relative rates of inflation in the countries concerned. Hence, argue the Anglo-Saxon sceptics, the EMS will not work, because the disparities between the participants' inflation rates are too great. No, the EMS will work, reply its sponsors, because it will foster the convergence of the underlying economic conditions in the participants' economies.

The first thing to be noted about the link between exchange rates and inflation rates is that it is only valid in the long or medium term, an expression which is suitably vague. In any period of time that is less than that, and this can mean up to a few years, divergent inflation rates can coexist perfectly well with a degree of exchange rate stability; beyond this period, the EMS is not meant to preclude, and in practice has not precluded, timely and necessary exchange rate adjustments. According to Christopher McMahon of the Bank of England[3]:

> 'The differing rates of inflation are usually mentioned as the greatest difficulty. But I think this problem can be exaggerated. Quite a wide divergence of inflation rates existed among members of the snake almost from its start, but they have managed to cope with this by reasonably frequent realignments.'

Experience since the entry into force of the EMS in March 1979 suggests that divergent inflation rates and relative exchange rate stability are compatible, in reality if not in theory. The Italian lira, for example, has remained in the EMS, despite a much higher rate of inflation in Italy than in the Federal Republic of Germany or the Benelux countries. *The compensating factor, neglected in theoretical discussions, has been interest rate differentials.* A very high rate of interest may not last for ever. But in the medium or long term, either the policy of high interest rates and monetary restraint works and inflation abates, or exchange rate adjustments may become necessary, following which, provided they take place in a timely and de-dramatized way, the EMS may still continue to function smoothly. It appears that lessons have been learnt from the past, and that the two currency adjustments that took place within the EMS in 1979 (devaluation of the Danish krone and revaluation of the German mark) did take place in a de-dramatized and low-key fashion.

Moreover, whether divergent inflation rates are compatible with exchange rate stability depends, as Professor Fritz Machlup has shown, on what is meant by exchange rate stability (see diagram)[4]. Thus, line A depicts greater stability than line B in the short term (day to day, week to week, or month to month), but greater instability in the long term. What does one mean by exchange rate stability, then? To be made precise and meaningful, this expression needs to be accompanied by indications of the time horizon aimed at and of the frequency and amplitude of the fluctuations.

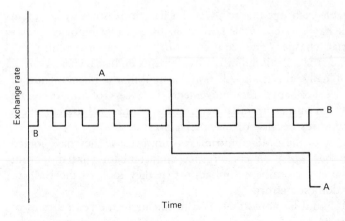

Exchange rate stability: short-term (A) or long-term (B)

Why is convergence important?

If, as has been argued, the EMS can tolerate a certain degree of divergence in inflation rates, why do the promoters of the EMS insist so emphatically on the need for convergence?

The first reason is that the Federal Republic of Germany, for the reasons that were analysed in Chapter Two, is extremely anxious to combat inflation everywhere and to prompote the 'convergence of economic policies'. Since the Federal Republic is likely to provide a major share of the financial resources of the EMS, it is natural that it should attempt to use the EMS as a vehicle for its designs.

Secondly, both the Benelux countries and France have converged towards the German philosophy. Thus, already in 1976, a former Belgian Minister wrote[5]:

> 'Inflation is the principal evil. ... Our will of rigour is expressed in our determination to remain unshakeably within the European monetary snake, i.e. not to allow ourselves to be distanced from the farsighted policy conducted by our German neighbours and partners' [my translation – Y. S. H.].

Since M Raymond Barre became Prime Minister, the French Government has apparently moved towards attaching higher priority to the control of inflation, in order to sanitize the economy and to help with the redeployment and restructuring of industry.

Thirdly, the causation runs not only from inflation to the exchange rate, but also from the exchange rate to inflation. A depreciating exchange rate adds to the momentum of inflation by making imports dearer (including raw materials); a stable exchange rate removes this dangerous spiral, whereas an appreciating exchange rate dampens inflation by making imported goods and raw materials cheaper. The requirement of exchange rate stability can help to strengthen the self-discipline of governments in their management of the economy. Finally, the EMS will assist in fighting the phenomenon of overshooting, i.e. exchange rate movements in excess of inflation rate differentials, which pushes up inflation rates in countries whose currences overshoot downwards because of speculative pressures.

Thus, for many of the EMS countries, it is not because they have joined the EMS that they insist on convergence and combating inflation, but because they insist on combating inflation that they look to the EMS to reinforce their domestic efforts.

Fourthly, it should be noted that, if adjustments in the central rates of EMS currencies become too frequent, the credibility of the system can be undermined.

Fifthly, to make the ECU attractive in relation to the US dollar, its purchasing power must be better preserved. This means that the overall inflation rate of the EMS zone should be lower than in the USA, which requires (within the EMS zone) convergence of the inflation rates towards the lower end.

The indicator of divergence

With the chorus of calls for convergence, it is not surprising that the indicator of divergence should be considered the major invention in the exchange rate mechanism of the EMS. It was designed to show whether one of the currencies was developing in a markedly different manner from the others and was hence responsible for tensions in the grid of bilateral parities (see appendix to this chapter). The justification for the device in terms of a compromise on the issue of symmetry between the burdens and obligations of the participants[6] is, however, misleading. For it is not true to say that, in the alternative, parity-grid system, the responsibility for intervention lies solely with the weaker currency if it has reached its lower intervention limit in relation to a strong currency. The strong and weak currencies will, by definition, have reached their bilateral margins simultaneously, and both central banks will have to intervene to maintain these margins. It is true that the central bank with the weaker currency will have to run down its foreign exchange reserves to do this, whereas the central bank with the stronger currency will be accumulating foreign exchange reserves, and that there is asymmetry in this. The country with the stronger currency, however, will be increasing its domestic money supply, and it can argue that this also represents a serious burden.

The indicator of divergence represented a method of reconciling the divergent interests of the Federal Republic of Germany, whose currency was expected to continue to appreciate, and the other countries, whose currencies were expected to continue to depreciate *vis-à-vis* the Deutschmark. The situation which the promotors of the EMS had in mind was as follows. Imagine that, because of a renewed weakness of the US dollar, there is a massive switch from dollars to the DM. The DM then rises in value in relation to the currencies of its EMS partners, and this appreciation has nothing to do with any divergence of performance between the EMS countries and currencies. Nevertheless, when the DM reaches its upper bilateral margin *vis-à-vis* the other EMS currencies, their central banks will, under the grid system, all have to intervene to pull the DM down and to pull their own currencies up. Thus, through no fault of their own, they will find themselves under the obligation to intervene. Alternatively, if intervention margins are defined in terms of the ECU, the situation described above may well result in the Bundesbank having to do all the intervention without the other EMS central banks being involved, since the DM may be diverging from the ECU without the other curencies so diverging.

During the negotiations leading to the inauguration of the EMS, the Germans insisted on the parity-grid system for defining intervention limits and hence responsibilities for taking action, while the other countries pressed for the currency-basket system. In the end, a compromise was adopted, whereby the obligatory intervention limits are defined, as the Germans wanted, bilaterally in terms of the parity grid, but in addition a divergence indicator was added to the system. When a currency crosses its threshold of divergence, which is defined in terms of the ECU (see appendix to this chapter), there is a *presumption* that the authorities concerned will correct the situation by adequate measures, including market intervention, measures of domestic monetary policy, changes in central rates, and other measures of economic policy. If such measures are not taken by the diverging currency's authorities, the reasons for this shall be given to the other authorities, especially in the concertation between the central banks.

The indicator of divergence also serves as an early warning system, since each currency's divergence threshold is set at 75 per cent of its maximum possible divergence *vis-à-vis* all other EMS currencies. A currency will normally cross its divergence threshold before it reaches its bilateral limits.

How the divergence indicator will work out in practice is not so much a technical as a political question. The sharing out of burdens will depend on the political commitment of each participant to the success of the EMS.

Summary and conclusions

If the major force behind the EMS is a convergence of interests *vis-à-vis* the problems raised by the paper-dollar standard, which is seen as having caused serious economic, financial and commercial losses to the Europeans, the centre-piece of the system is the ECU and its institutional underpinning, the EMF, both of which have not yet assumed a definitive modality and are still in the process of evolution. In this context, the question of exchange rates between EMS currencies assumes a secondary importance, and is important only to the extent that exchange rate stability between EMS currencies is necessary for the promotion of the international use of the ECU. At the technical level, exchange rate stability, depending on what it means, is compatible with divergent inflation rates, the compensating mechanism in the short term being interest rate differentials, and in the longer term, timely exchange rate adjustments. If divergence of inflation rates is not such an insurmountable difficulty, the question arises as to why convergence is made into such an issue. It is not because the Federal Republic of Germany, the Benelux countries and France have joined the EMS that they insist on controlling inflation; it is because they are keen to control inflation that they look to the EMS to reinforce national efforts.

The divergence indicator is the result of a political compromise; its functioning will depend on the political commitment of the EMS participants.

The Mechanisms of the European Monetary System

The mechanisms of the EMS fall into three parts: the exchange rate mechanism; the European Currency Unit (ECU); and the first steps towards the European Monetary Fund (EMF).

The exchange rate mechanism

Each currency has a central rate defined in terms of the ECU. These central rates are used to establish a grid of bilateral exchange rates. All EEC currencies (except the pound, which does not participate in the exchange rate mechanisms, and the lira, which enjoys wider margins of 6 per cent) must keep within fluctuation margins of 2.25 per cent in relation to each of the other currencies. The 2.25 per cent margins constitute compulsory intervention points.

The divergence indicator is an additional system, and is defined in terms of the ECU. Each currency has a maximum divergence *spread* in relation to the ECU which would theoretically be reached when it reached the limits of all its bilateral margins *vis-à-vis* other currencies. The divergence *threshold* is set at 75 per cent of this maximum divergence spread. The divergence spreads and thresholds are so calculated as to eliminate the impact of the different gravitational pull of the currencies on the ECU.

When a currency crosses its divergence threshold, a presumption is established that action will be taken by the authorities concerned. If not, explanations have to be given. The exchange rate system therefore combines mandatory bilateral intervention limits and a presumption to act when the divergence threshold is reached, normally earlier.

The European Currency Unit

The ECU is a basket of the nine EEC currencies. The weight of each currency in the ECU depends on the country's share in intra-Community trade, share in total Community GDP, and quotas in the financial and credit mechanisms under the EMS. The weights are fixed but can be revised from time to time.

An initial supply of ECUs has been created by the European Monetary Co-operation Fund (EMCF) against the deposit by each of the nine central banks of 20 per cent of its gold and dollar reserves. There is a special formula for the valuation of gold. The deposits take the form of renewable three-month swap arrangements. The next logical step will be to consolidate these swaps into a more permanent arrangement.

Initially the ECU is being used as a *numéraire* for defining the exchange rates, the divergence indicator, etc. and as a means of settlement between the EEC central banks. The next logical step will be to extend the use, particularly in international transactions, of the ECU.

The European Monetary Fund

The resolution of the European Council which met in Brussels in December 1978 stated:

'We remain firmly resolved to consolidate, not later than two years after the start of the scheme, into a final system the provisions and procedures thus created. This system will entail the creation of the European Monetary Fund as announced in the conclusions of the European Council meeting at Bremen on 6/7 July 1978, as well as the full utilization of the ECU as a reserve asset and a means of settlement. It will be based on adequate legislation at the Community as well as at the national level.'

It should be noted that, despite this statement, President Giscard d'Estaing and Chancellor Schmidt appear to have agreed, in the course of 1980, to put off the move to the next phase, for domestic political reasons. Once again, progress in Community schemes depended on what were perceived to be domestic interests.

Meanwhile, the very short-term financing facility, the short-term monetary support, and the medium-term financial assistance are strengthened by either increasing the amounts available or lengthening the duration of the credits. Italy and Ireland are to receive special interest-relief grants in connection with Community loans, in order to facilitate their adhesion to the EMS.

1 The unorthodox view concentrates less on the exchange-rate technicalities and looks at the broader, politico-economic picture. See: Robert Triffin, 'The international role and fate of the dollar', *Foreign Affairs*, winter 1978/9; Daniel Biron and Alexandre Faire, 'Le mark souverain', *Le Monde diplomatique*, November 1978.

2 Triffin, op. cit.

3 Christopher McMahon, 'The long-run implications of the EMS', in Philip H. Trezise (ed.), *The European Monetary System: Its Promises and Prospects*, Washington DC, The Brookings Institution, 1979.

4 Fritz Machlup, 'The EMS, the odds for stability, the US dollar, and the IMF', *Aussenwirtschaft*, March 1979.

5 F. Herman, 'Le Marché commun et les états membres face à la crise économique, *Studia diplomatica*, No. 6, 1976.

6 The Commission of the European Communities, (article on the EMS), *European Economy*, July 1979.

Bibliographical note

Because the EMS is of such recent origin, the reader must consult mainly articles and conference papers on the subject. The articles by R. Triffin in *Foreign Affairs*, op. cit., and also in P. H. Tresize, op. cit., and by Biron and Faire, op. cit., give a good analysis of the historical background of the EMS in terms of German and French interests and motivations. See also: 'The European Monetary System: structure and operation', *Monthly Report of the Deutsche Bundesbank*, March 1979; 'Présentation du Systéme Monétaire Européen', *Bulletin trimestriel de la Banque de France*, March 1979; 'The European Monetary System, commentary and documents', *European Economy*, July 1979; and D. C. Kruse, *Monetary Integration in Western Europe: EMU, EMS and beyond*, London, Butterworth, 1980.

The Promotion of Convergence and Financial Prospects for the Community

In this chapter, convergence refers to economic growth and income levels. The debate about the convergence of economic performance or achievements in this sense inevitably brings us to the issue of Community finances.

Can and should the Community promote convergence?

Conceptually, there is a fundamental difference between a real and sustainable convergence of income levels as a result of a faster rate of self-sustaining economic growth in the less prosperous countries, and the propping up of income and consumption levels through financial transfers that may do little or nothing to raise the rate of economic growth and the level or productivity in the recipient country or region. Financial transfers may be directed towards the maintenance of consumption and current expenditure by the government, or they may be directed towards infrastructural and productive investments and thus the raising of the growth and productivity potential in the recipient country or region.

In theory, all member states agree that if the Community is to promote convergence, it is real and sustainable convergence that should be promoted. However, economic growth has its own momentum and depends on a variety of economic, political, social and cultural factors, many of which are not directly amenable to government policy. If national governments, with their panoply of powers and instruments and dealing with integrated national economies, find it difficult to influence the rate of economic growth, what can be expected from the European Community? The European Council, meeting in Brussels in December 1978, answered this question, among others, by stating:

'... We are aware that the convergence of economic policies and of economic performance will not be easy to achieve. Therefore, steps must be taken to strengthen the economic potential of the less prosperous countries of the Community. This is primarily the responsibility of the member states concerned. Community measures can and should serve a supporting role.'

This position was repeated in the Conclusions of the Presidency of the Paris meeting of European Council in March 1979:

'... Achievement of the convergence of the economic performance requires measures for which the Member States concerned are primarily responsible, but in respect of which Community policies can and must play a supporting role within the framework of increased solidarity.'

At its present stage of evolution, there are not many means by which the Community can help. The two main categories are financial transfers and permitted derogations from the EEC's competition and trade rules. In the early years of the EEC, there was a current of liberal economic thinking which believed that the mere functioning of the Common Market would, through free trade, competition and free factor movements, be sufficient to ensure convergence. (According to neo-classical economic theory, the countries with an abundance of labour would specialize in the production and export of labour-intensive products. This would raise wage levels. In addition, capital would flow into these countries, and labour emigration would be a further help.) Even today, there are some who argue that member states' commitment in the Treaty of Rome to 'strengthen the unity of their economies and to ensure their harmonious development by reducing the differences existing between the various regions and the backwardness of the less favoured regions' (Treaty Preamble) is to be attained, as far as the Community is concerned, by 'establishing a common market and progressively approximating the economic policies of the Member States', as indicated in Article 2 of the treaty, rather than through financial transfers[1]. Such an extreme position probably represents only a minority view. More than twenty years of the Common Market has not resulted in a significant reduction of regional disparities in the Community as a whole. Convergence therefore brings us inevitably to the question of resource transfers (since the alternative is derogations from EEC rules, which are regarded as dangerous for the Common Market, and tend to be authorized only as temporary measures in times of national crisis or in connection with previously agreed and Community-monitored programmes of adjustment and restructuring).

Large-scale financial transfers simply to prop up consumption levels are unacceptable to rich countries all over the world, and the European Community is no exception to this principle of financial orthodoxy. In its view, such transfers would amount to helping those who do not help themselves, and the EEC would risk degenerating into a 'transfer union'[2], a community of *assistés*, of social-welfare recipients. This would undermine self-discipline and the work ethic, and would jeopardize the survival of Europe in a competitive world. Moreover, if financial transfers are undertaken for the purpose of income and consumption support, there would be no end to the process in time, and, if the disparities between richer and poorer countries continued to widen, the amounts to be transferred would grow continuously and indefinitely. The MacDougall report[3] recognized that redistribution is, by definition, of a continuing nature (p. 12), but does not appear to have addressed itself to the question of the continuous rise in the amounts that would have to be transferred.

The position of the richer EEC member states, the Federal Republic of Germany in particular, is that the European Community is not a political union and that the degree of intra-Community integration, solidarity and consensus attained is insufficient to justify large-scale financial transfers as an end in itself (i.e. to prop up income and consumption levels in the name of equity and solidarity). Financial transfers, if they take place within the EEC, should be undertaken as a means to Community ends, including the promotion of Community cohesion and the achievement of a greater degree of monetary stability[4]. Financial transfers undertaken in the name of convergence should be strictly controlled (if possible) and directed only towards investment and the raising of the recipients' growth and productivity potential. Finally, Community loans are at least as useful as budgetary transfers or grants (I shall come back to this point). Sometimes it is also argued that, as the example of the USA shows, a common market and the subsistence of regional income differentials are perfectly compatible.

The arguments advanced by the Federal Republic of Germany are difficult to refute on their own grounds, in part because of their apparent sweet reasonableness, and in part because it is the Federal Republic which, in the last analysis, will have to pay for the transfers. There is, however, a totally different kind of approach, which has been adopted by the United Kingdom and Italy.

The argument starts from a judgement that European integration has reached a stage where inter-country transfers have become significant (in relation to trade balances and the amounts that governments are trying to cut from their expenditures, if not in relation to GDP), and can no longer be ignored. Thus the Community is already engaged in the business of effecting transfers, albeit incidentally and in the name of the CAP. Moreover, these transfers are totally perverse in that they flow or have flown from the poorer member states to the richer ones instead of the other way round. Both Italy, the second poorest member state, and the United Kingdom, the third poorest, have been net contributors to the Community budget, whereas the Benelux countries and Denmark, which have per-capita income levels (at both current exchange rates and purchasing-power parities) at or close to the top of the EEC range, have been enjoying net receipts from the Community budget which were quite large in per-capita terms. (Ireland is also a large net recipient, in per-capita terms, but these receipts are not regarded as perverse inasmuch as Ireland has been – until the accession of Greece – the poorest member state.) Perverse resource flows, however, are not only a matter of budgetary transfers. The United Kingdom and Italy are also net importers of agricultural products and, under the CAP, they have to pay more for these than what they would have had to pay if the CAP did not exist or if they left the CAP. On imports from outside the EEC, the higher prices are reflected in the budgetary figures through the import levies, but on intra-Community trade, which is free from levies, they do not show up in budgetary flows at all.

The concept that net agricultural exporting countries benefit and that net agricultural importing countries suffer because of the high level of prices maintained by the CAP is fairly straightforward, but any attempt to measure these 'trade transfers' runs into the methodological problem of what to take as the alternative position, as the basis for comparison with the actual situation. Most studies have taken 'world prices'[5]. The trouble is that there is no such thing as a single world price for any given commodity, that world prices are highly unstable, and that if the EEC as a whole were to supply its food requirements from world markets on any significant scale, world prices would rise. This has led to an ingenious attempt[6] to measure the 'trade transfers' (as distinct from the budgetary ones) by assuming that the same support mechanisms and the same price levels as under the CAP are applied in each of the member states, but this time through national support policies, without the principles of financial solidarity and Community preference. Since, by definition, world supply, demand and prices are not affected, the current levels of export restitutions and import levies can be used as indications of the trade transfers. Whatever the methodologies adopted, the losers on the trade transfers include two of the poorest members of the European Community, Italy and the United Kingdom, while wealthy Netherlands and Denmark figure prominently among the gainers.

Thus the operation of Community policies engenders perverse transfers, through the budget and intra-Community trade, from two poor countries, the United Kingdom and Italy, to net agricultural exporters in the EEC, many of whom (Denmark, the Netherlands, Belgium, Luxembourg and France) have income levels near or at the top of the EEC league. This situation provides a powerful answer to the questions whether the Community can and should promote convergence. The Community can indeed promote convergence by putting a stop to the perverse transfers which reduce income levels and economic well-being in the poorer member states and hence accentuate divergence. The Community should do this, it can be argued, because the situation is unjust, perverse, and politically untenable.

Leaving aside the argument of perverse transfers, one can detect (cf. the MacDougall report[3]) more than half a dozen justifications for intra-Community redistribution. It may be considered to be a political objective of the Community; it may be needed to prevent excessive migrations of both general and skilled labour (but it should be noted that most of the migration in the EEC has been from outside countries and that intra-Community migration represents less than 2 per cent of the total domestic working population of the Nine – although internal migration may become more important after the second enlargement to include Greece, Spain and Portugal); it is needed to assist the productivity and competitiveness of the poorer members and to help them contain inflation; it is needed to support or underpin a monetary union, to compensate for the loss at national level of a number of instruments of economic policy and to safeguard against an uneven distribution of the costs and benefits of integration; there is a political expectation that the Community should help with the acute problems of the day; the Community has a responsibility for the effects of integration and for the absence of national trade policies; finally, the Community has an interest in avoiding beggar-my-neighbour policies that adversely affect other member states.

What these arguments fail to address is why the richer member states, in particular the Federal Republic of Germany, should dig into their pockets. The Federal Republic, like any other normal country, will be willing to pay only to the extent that the cost is commensurate with the expected benefits. Such benefits may well be perceived and defined in terms of the preservation of the Common Market, of free trade, of European political co-operation and of the EMS, but there must be a limit to the burden that the Federal Republic is willing and able to assume. It is, for example, not in the interests of the Federal Republic to allow itself to be so weakened by what it considers to be the nagging demands of weaker partners that its ability to compete in the ruthless world of international competition is jeopardized. Moreover, the fact that Germany is capable of surviving alone in global competition may reduce the value of the EEC for it. As for the EMS, the argument sometimes appears to be that participation in the EMS is not only not a burden, but is good for the participants in promoting stability and growth and the control of inflation. There is then no need, the argument runs, to compensate the weaker members for any non-existent losses, except perhaps for the transitional problems that may accompany a change towards greater stability. In any case, the ability of the Federal Republic to pay for its EEC partners may have been seriously eroded by the emergence of a current-account deficit in 1980 (see below), domestic pressures on government spending, and other, overseas, commitments (e.g. to Turkey, Poland, NATO).

The impact of the UK budgetary settlement

Whatever the ability and willingness of the Federal Republic of Germany to pay for its partners may have been, they have been considerably reduced by the agreement of 30 May 1980 on the UK budgetary problem. The reduction in the United Kingdom's net contributions of 2585 million ECUs/EUAs for the two years 1980 and 1981 (1175 million in 1980 and 1410 million in

1981) will be shared out between the other member states according to the Own Resources mechanism. According to Commission estimates made in June 1980, the Federal Republic will bear 39.1 per cent of the burden, followed by France at 30.1 per cent (see *Table 9.1*).

Table 9.1 *Contributions to the British settlement, 1980 and 1981 (in million ECU/EUAs)*[1]

Belgium	139	Ireland	25
Denmark	75	Italy	375
France	778	Luxembourg	6
Federal Republic of Germany	1011	Netherlands	175
		Total	2585

1. 1 ECU = DM2.51 = $1.42 = £0.6.
Source: Embassy of the Federal Republic of Germany, *Report from the Federal Republic of Germany*, London, 11 June 1980.

Table 9.2 *Net contributions to the Community (budget in millions ECUs)*

	1980		1981	
	From	*To*	*From*	*To*
Federal Republic of Germany	−1192	−1725	−1360	−1978
France	+15	−365	+10	−355
United Kingdom	−1784	−623	−2140	−783

Source: Embassy of the Federal Republic of Germany, *Report from the Federal Republic of Germany*, London, 11 June 1980.

According to another set of estimates by the Federal Ministry of Finance in Bonn, the UK settlement will alter the net contribution to the Community budget of the Federal Republic, France and the United Kingdom as shown in *Table 9.2*

The Federal Republic may no longer be in a position to support such a burden even for a few years, however, because of the recent emergence of a current-account deficit, which was forecast to total DM28 000 million, or 11 000 million ECUs, in 1980 and which is not likely to disappear quickly. In comparison with 11 000 million ECUs, a net budgetary contribution of almost 2000 million ECUs per year is certainly not insignificant. Probably for the first time, France is also becoming an important net contributor as a result of the settlement. There is therefore likely to be intense and combined Franco-German pressure against any increase in resource tranfers to other member states, be it in the name of convergence or whatever.

Community finances

The UK budget settlement intervenes in the context of the imminent exhaustion of the Community's Own Resources. This latter situation results from developments both in receipts and expenditure.

As for receipts, agricultural levies have been stagnant because imports of agricultural products from outside the EEC have been strongly discouraged by the CAP; import duties are growing only very slowly because of the world-wide reduction in tariff rates as a result of successive trade negotiations under the auspices of GATT; this leaves value-added tax (VAT) contributions to bridge the remaining gap between expenditure and levies and duties. The VAT contributions, however, cannot exceed the 1 per cent ceiling (of each member state's harmonized VAT base) without parliamentary approval in each member state. The odds are that the national parliaments are likely to make such approval very difficult. The increase in the burden of taxation has become a universal complaint in most Western countries. An increase in Community taxation at a time when governments are everywhere having to cut their expenditures is likely to be even more unpopular, especially in the United Kingdom, which will remain a large net contributor to the Community budget and where anti-European feelings may run high, and in the Federal Republic of Germany, which sees itself as the Community's milch cow and resents this role strongly. In any case, the government of the Federal Republic, France and the United Kingdom have publicly announced that the 1 per cent ceiling must not be exceeded.

On the expenditure side, CAP spending through the EAGGF has consistently accounted for three-quarters of the total and has grown year after year. There is a complicated array of reasons for this, including productivity increases of the order of around 10 per cent per year; the open-ended obligation under the CAP to purchase unlimited amounts of CAP products, at intervention prices, for storage; the setting of CAP prices at levels that have failed to deter production; and the rules of the game governing the behaviour of the agricultural ministers meeting as the Council. These rules have been picturesquely described in terms of the elevator (Minister A wants to extract the maximum gains for his farmers, so he supports Minister B in B's maximum efforts in return for B's support, and so on) and of ordering lobsters (if a group of people are going to share the bill, why should each exercise restraint and not order lobster?). On top of all this, the UK budgetary settlement can only advance the day when Own Resources will run out.

The agreement of 30 may 1980 states:

'... For 1982, the Community is pledged to resolve the problem by means of structural changes (Commission mandate). The examination should concern the development of Community policies, without calling into question the common financial responsibility for these policies, which are financed from the Community's own resources, or the basic principles of the Common Agricultural Policy. ...

The Council reaffirm the conclusions adopted by it on 11 February 1980 which included reference to the 1 per cent VAT own resources ceiling. ....'

Basically speaking, there are two approaches towards solving the agri-budgetary problem. The first is directly through the Community budget, by introducing ceilings or upper limits on net contributions as well as net receipts by individual countries and/or conditionality clauses in relation to these. The Federal Republic of Germany, the largest net contributor, and France, which has now joined the ranks of net contributors, are fully aware that the net beneficiaries include some extremely wealthy countries (Belgium, Denmark and the Netherlands). The British case was based *inter alia* on the fact that it is the third poorest member state. A precedent has now been established, and the argument can be extended: why should some of the wealthiest member states be large net recipients?

The second approach is to control expenditure, particularly CAP expenditure. Because cutting the prices of CAP products is such a political taboo that member states would rather risk the breakdown of the system than accept such cuts, the methods of controlling CAP expenditure must be indirect, and include the co-responsibility levy, quanta and quotas, supplemented by direct income support in lieu of price support in certain cases. The great difficulty will be the distribution of the costs between the member states.

The control of CAP expenditure is part of a much wider issue than the exhaustion of the 1 per cent ceiling. If CAP expenditure is slowed down, this would release resources for other Community policies. What will be at stake in a couple of years' time is the balance of Community policies, the distribution of costs and benefits between member states, the readjustment of the *status quo*, and the future orientation of the Community.

Community loans

The budgetary constraints facing both the Community and most of its national governments give a much greater relevance to the use of Community loans to promote convergence. Inter-country financial transfers can take the form of grants (from the budget) or loans. Community loans take the form of ECSC loans, European Investment Bank (EIB) loans, Euratom loans, EEC loans for balance-of-payments assistance, loans from the New Community Instrument (the Ortoli facility), etc. The most important channel is the EIB. A few comparisons can give an idea of the relative importance of Community loans as an instrument to promote convergence.

In 1978, budgetary appropriations for the European Regional Development Fund (ERDF) amounted to 525 milliion EUAs and for the Social Fund 539 million EUAs, whereas the EIB provided around 2000 million EUAs of financing for projects located within the EEC, and ECSC loans amounted to 800 million EUAs. The ratio of EIB to ERDF financing was almost 4 to 1. In 1979, total Community lending amounted to 3600 million EUAs[7]. This compares with a total European Community budget of 14 447 million EAUs, a ratio of 1 to 4, but total budgetary spending on all purposes other than the CAP amounted to only 3731 million EUAs, which was roughly equal to total Community lending in that year.

The European Communities have been in the business of effecting inter-country resource transfers long before the ERDF was established in 1975. In the negotiations leading up to the signing of the Treaty of Rome, the Italians sought assistance for the Mezzogiorno, but the Germans refused to allow the mechanism to be called a fund, which for them is synonymous with the wastage of public money, and insisted that it should be called a bank – even if the Member States initially had to contribute largely to its capital – in order to emphasize their determinations to pursue economic rationality and efficiency[8]. The statute of the EIB was an integral part of the Treaty of Rome (Articles 129 and 130 and the annexed Protocol), and the bank began its first financing operations in 1959. In 1961, the bank made its first bond issues on the capital markets. The ECSC was created even earlier, in 1951, with borrowing and lending powers.

Given, then, the existence of the EIB as an instrument for promoting development and convergence, which by 1973 had reached an annual lending of 700 million EUAs within the Community, why did the Germans agree to the setting up of the ERDF in response to the post-enlargement pressure of the United Kingdom, Italy and Ireland? One of the reasons was probably that the EIB lends only for *projects*, while it could be argued that the consolidation of integration and Community cohesion would in addition be helped by regional development *programmes*, consisting of a package of mutually reinforcing projects and which would provide for the review and improvement of government regional *policies* within the context of the Community as a whole. Thus, not only would regional programmes supplement the traditional project approach, but a beginning would be made with a genuine Community regional policy which would bring the regions into direct contact with the Community.

In the event, this was not to be so. The opposition of France and the United Kingdom ensured that Community regional aids can only be disbursed through national governments for projects presented only by them. There was considerable German disappointment at discovering that the British saw the ERDF largely in terms of balancing out its contributions to the Community budget[9]. The weight to be accorded to British demands was further diminished by the UK stance on energy questions and the renegotiations. But the European Commission, Italy and Ireland continued to press for the establishment of the ERDF, and the result was a much smaller fund than had been hoped by many.

Thus, the ERDF was never able to match up to the loan instruments. EIB loans for Community projects continued their rapid growth, from 700 million EUAs in 1973, the year of enlargement, to 2000 million EUAs in 1978, during which year it was decided to double its capital base. Between 1973 and 1978, 70 per cent of the EIB's loans in the EEC were for infrastructure and energy, the rest for industry, including loans channelled through banks in the member states.

It is often thought that grants are more valuable than loans because the former do not have to be repaid. However, the discipline that industrial development banking imposes on project appraisal, project evaluation and project execution, a discipline that can act as an umbrella against political interference by national and local governments motivated by electoral considerations, and that can act to screen out unviable projects, may well be its most valuable contribution. The less prosperous regions may lack not only capital for investment purposes, but also project-implementation and project-supervision capability and an industrial banking tradition (in contrast with short-term commercial banking). The United Kingdom may not lack financial resources, but there is a distinction between these in general and financial resources available on the right terms for long-term investment purposes[10]. In addition, one of the major problems in the United Kingdom is that public-sector investment projects are delayed or chopped according to the political cycle and economic stop–go; Community grants channelled through the government will not protect these projects from such stop–go and political interference, but EIB loans directly to the project entities would.

The more prosperous countries naturally prefer to adopt the banking rather than the budgetary approach. First, the money is raised on the capital markets, thus avoiding a call on the exchequer and the taxpayer in the wealthy countries. Secondly, financial discipline will (it is hoped) be imposed. Thirdly, the loans go ostensibly to investment projects, not consumption. Fourthly, as a corollary, there will be something to show for the loans. Fifthly, well-selected and designed projects, by contributing to the developing of the recipient country, should (it is hoped) eventually eliminate the need for assistance, whereas income transfers may have to continue indefinitely to support people unable to help themselves.

Summary and conclusions

The arguments for the promotion of the convergence of economic performance fail to address themselves to the question why the richer countries, the

Federal Republic of German in particular, should dig into their pockets. Moreover, there is not too much that the Community can do to promote a real convergence based on faster, self-sustaining growth in the less prosperous member states, since growth depends on many factors not amenable to policy. The Community can effect transfers designed to raise the growth and productivity potential of the recipient regions through investments, it can permit derogations to EEC rules of competition and trade, and perhaps more important, it can remove a source of divergence by putting an end to the perverse trade and budgetary transfers from the poor to the rich. Transfers as an end in themselves or to prop up consumption are out of the question.

The impact of the UK budgetary settlement is to increase Germany's net contribution significantly at a time when it is beginning to experience a current-account deficit, to turn France into a net contributor of some importance, and to hasten the day when the Community runs out of Own Resources.

There are two approaches to a solution of the agri-budgetary problem: either directly through the budget, by introducing limits on net contributions and receipts, or by reform of the CAP. Both could have major implications for the future of the Community.

The budgetary constraints facing the Community and the national governments add to the relevance of Community loans as an instrument for promoting convergence. In 1978, EIB loans were almost four times ERDF appropriations. The major value of loans may lie in the discipline that they impose.

1 According to a German economist from the Kiel Institute of World Economics: '... it would be hard to show that redistribution policies were also intended by the treaty [of Rome]. Moreover, if reducing per capita income differences among the member countries by income redistribution had been aimed at, this could have been reached more effectively by a Community-wide system of financial compensation than by the variety of common policies which has been introduced. ... There may very well be good reasons for nations to choose slow economic progress. But equally there may be good reasons for other countries to opt for fast growth and rapid change. Given such a constellation, why then should faster growing economies compensate the slower growing ones?' (Carsten Thoroe, 'Comment', in: W. Wallace (ed.), *Britain in Europe*, London, Heinemann, 1980).
2 See, for example, Dieter Biehl, 'The

impact of enlargement on regional development and regional policy in the EC', in H. Wallace and I. Hevremann (eds.), *A Community of Twelve? The Impact of Further Enlargement on the EC*, Bruges, 1978. Biehl wrote: 'Trying to transform the Community into a pure and simple "Transfer Union" would certainly risk to lose soon the support of large political groups and of a large majority of citizens who are still waiting for more political progress in European integration.'
3 Commission of the European Communities, *Report of the Study Group on the Role of Public Finance in European Integration*, Brussels, April 1977.
4 See, for example, a speech by Helmut Schmidt, published in the *Financial Times*, 2 January 1979.
5 Paolo Blancus. 'The CAP and the balance of payments of the EEC member countries' *Banca Nazionale del Lavoro*

Quarterly Review, December 1978; and 'Policies of the EEC', *Cambridge Economic Policy Review*, April 1979.
6 J. M. C. Rollo and K. S. Warwick, *The CAP and Resource Flows among EEC Member States*, London, Government Economic Service, 1979 (Working Paper 27).
7 *European Economy*, July 1980.

8 J. F. Deniau, *L'Europe interdite*, Paris, 1977, p. 81.
9 Helen Wallace in: H. Wallace (ed.) *et al.*, *Policy-Making in the European Communities*, Chichester, John Wiley, 1977.
10 This has been argued in Y.S. Hu, *National Attitudes and the Financing of Industry*, London, PEP, 1976.

Bibliographical note

In addition to what is contained in the notes above, the reader may want to consult: Commission of the European Communities, *Reference Document on Budgetary Questions*, Brussels, September 1979 (COM(79)462); D. Strasser, *Les Finances de l'Europe*, Paris, Presses Universitaires de France, 1975; F. Franzmeyer and B. Seidel, *Überstaatlicher Finanzausgleich und Europäische Integration*, Bonn, Europa Union Verlag, 1976; D. Biehl, 'Determinants of regional disparities and the role of public finance', *Public Finance* (The Hague), No. 1, 1980; W. Wallace, *Budgetary Politics: the Finances of the ECs*, London, Allen & Unwin, 1980; 'The structural funds of the European Communities', *European Economy*, July 1980.

Concluding Remarks

Divergence and the theory of integration

In a sense, divergence has become a problem only because the European Community is not (or not yet) an integrated whole. About provinces in a unitary State, for example, one may talk of disparities, but not of divergence. The notion of divergence implies some autonomy, some independence, and some capacity to exercise the option of going one's own way.

The neo-functionalist theory of integration may be thought of as being based on two major assumptions. The first was purely economic and stated that the removal of trade and other barriers between the member states of the EEC would lead to the progressive fusion of their economies. The second premise concerned the relationship between the political and the economic spheres and stated that the process of economic integration would spill over into a process of political integration and that economic union would be followed by political union. On both counts, the theory has so far proved too optimistic.

Take the economic premise first. The creation of a common market in industrial products has not resulted in the replacement of national industrial structures by a European industrial structure. Except for the European subsidiaries of the American multinational companies (which have been able, to a greater extent than the indigenous companies, to deploy and rationalize their activities and assets on a Europe-wide basis[1]) and except for a few binational companies such as Shell and Unilever which are Anglo-Dutch, companies and industries in the EEC are still owned and controlled nationally. Although they sell to and operate in many countries they remain German, French, British, Italian, etc., and the bulk of their fixed assets, usually more than half, is located in their home countries. When they need government support, they turn to their national governments rather than to a fictitious EEC authority. Mergers and rationalizations continue to take place predominantly on a national basis rather than on an EEC basis. In the 1960s, much hope had been generated by attempted transnational mergers such as those between Fiat-Citroën and Dunlop-Pirelli, but those attempts have come to nothing.

In a sense it is because industries remain nationally distinct, both in an objective sense and in the perceptions of national governments and of their populations that, despite the attempts of the EEC Commission[2], the common industrial policy is so little developed (some would say non-existent), for when industries retain their national identity, the question of divergences of national interests arises in the industrial field. We have seen (in Chapter 6) that, in declining industries such as steel, it is difficult to agree on the allocation of costs and cut-backs and hence to rationalize and restructure on an EEC basis. It stands to reason that agreement should be easier to obtain in the advanced-technology and fast-growth industries; the minimum scale required for commercial success is often very large, beyond the capacity of single European nations, while the growth of the market and the opportunity to snatch some market share from the market leaders (read, the Americans) mean that all the participants stand to gain from co-operation or integration. Yet the few projects that have materialized, of which the most successful one to date is probably the European Airbus, have been undertaken outside or without reference to the Community framework: the companies have been national companies, the government assistance has been national, and the markets have been a pooling of the national markets of the participating countries. This form of co-operation outside the Community framework has given rise to the formula of a variable-geometry Europe, to which I return later. What should be noted here is that this form of co-operation has been confined to specific projects and has not led to, and is not meant to lead to, a fusion of the firms involved.

So much for industry. In agriculture, despite the CAP, the Commission's detailed interventions, and the large sums of money spent on the CAP through the EAGGF, it is well to remember that national governments still spend, taking all the EC member states together, twice as much on their national agricultures as the EAGGF, that agricultural prices vary from one country to another (this is made possible in a technical sense by the MCAs, as we saw in Chapter 5), and that farm structures and farmers' incomes also vary considerably. In the face of these well-recognized facts, it is hard to pretend that there has been real integration in the agricultural sector.

It may be argued that the reason why market integration has not been followed by the integration of economic structures is that there are still many barriers to be removed. The complete removal of all of these 'non-tariff barriers' (as they are called) to the 'free circulation of goods, capital, people and services' would require, in my view, the eradication of the existence of nation-states. This brings us to the second major premise of the neo-functionalist theory of integration.

This appears to have been based on the view that the accretion of economic functions at the Commnity level and the spill-over from the economic to the political sphere would cumulatively and imperceptibly deprive the national governments of their *raison d'être* and would dissolve the phenomenon of the nation-state. Thus political union would be achieved through the back door, so to speak. However, as the Hungarian economist the late Imre Vajda stated[3]:

> 'The experience we have already gained of the process of integration certainly bears witness to the fact that the national state is strong and cannot easily be liquidated by integration. ... Economic union is not a stage on the path leading towards political union, but a possible and desirable consequence of the latter.'

I do not wish to be drawn into the thorny subject of the reasons for the continued existence and vitality of the phenomenon of the nation-state. It is possible, however, to conclude for our purposes. As long as economic structures remain nationally distinct and as long as the nation-state remains a live force, divergence between EC member states remains an actual or virtual problem, even if a long period of relative stability in the world environment (as in much of the 1950s and 1960s) may serve to mask or attenuate the problem; in particular, national interests and national perceptions remain distinct.

From a political point of view, the kinds of economic divergence that matter in the Community are the divergence of economic power and the divergence of perceived national interests, both between member states. These are related to the divergence of economic performance or developments.

Divergence of economic power

Divergence of economic power may result in a change in relative national power if the change in relative economic power is not offset by contrary changes in relative political or military power. An important change in relative national power in an alliance system can lead to serious strains in the system, because the balance of policies and interests, established on the basis of an earlier *rapport de forces*, will no longer correspond with the now altered distribution of power.

A good case in point concerns the formal distribution of power in the Council of the European Communities, the only Community institution with the power to adopt legal instruments (regulations, directives, decisions[4]) for the attainment of the Community's objectives. According to the Treaty of Rome, 'save as otherwise provided in this Treaty, the Council shall act by a majority of its members' (Article 148). The majority may be, according to circumstances, a simple or qualified majority. For a qualified majority, the four larger countries have 10 votes each, Belgium and the Netherlands 5 each, Denmark and Ireland 3 each, and Luxembourg 2; the qualified majority is 41 votes or more out of the total of 58. Thus, formally speaking, the Federal Republic of Germany is on a footing of equality with France, the United Kingdom and Italy for the purpose of calculating a qualified majority and accounts for 17 per cent of the total weighted votes, yet, at current prices and market exchange rates, it represents about 31 per cent of total Community GDP. This discrepancy has already caused some tension in the European Community system, and these tensions could easily escalate if and when the Federal Republic decides that it has had enough of behaving as 'the good boy' and 'being held to ransom' by its EEC partners.

In the European Monetary System as presently constituted, the decisions are taken by the Council of Ministers, with the same formal distribution of voting power as in any Council. Under the financing facility and the credit mechanisms, the Federal Republic has exactly the same debtor and creditor quotas as France, Italy and the United Kingdom. Yet when the EMS came into force in March/April 1979, Germany probably accounted for 42 per cent of all the new ECUs then created by the European Monetary Co-operation Fund[5], compared with 20 per cent for France. Available data since then do not permit the same calculations, but International Monetary Fund (IMF) data show that, in June 1980 for example, the Federal Republic represented 37 per cent of the total EEC holdings of foreign exchange and special drawing rights, compared with 20 per cent for France, 17 per cent for the United Kingdom, and 16 per cent for Italy; the Federal Republic also held 28 per cent of total EEC gold holdings, compared with 24 per cent for France, 19 per cent for Italy, and 5.5 per cent for the United Kingdom. The only point in the EMS at which there is some correspondence is in the weight of the Deutsche Mark in the ECU (33 per cent). A major question about the future EMF, about which very little is being said these days, is whether voting power will be distributed as in the Council or whether the EMF will follow the natural pattern set by the IMF, in which voting powers are determined according to each country's financial contribution. The people I talked to in the Federal Republic of Germany regard it as natural that relative voting power should be determined by relative financial exposure or relative economic weight.

Furthermore divergence in the sense of a continuous increase in the degree of disparity can cause serious psychological and hence political problems between close neighbours[6]:

> '... [Interdependence] puts into stark relief the unevenness of power. The closer the bonds, the more troublesome is inequality, for there will be a permanent temptation to exploit or reverse it. Interdependence among unequals is likely to be recurrently unbearable both to the very strong and to the very weak. It will be unacceptable to the very strong, if they are constantly summoned to make sacrifices on behalf of the weak and, so to speak, to subsidize them in order to prevent the system's unravelling, especially if such help would either save the weak from having to shape

up, or allow them to challenge their benefactor. ... And the terms of interdependence will be unacceptable to the weak, if they have means of redress. ... The growing discrepancy between Bonn and its partners within the EEC has resulted, if not in a breakdown of a Community that continues to serve the interests of all its members (Bonn has to keep its weaker partners from imposing unilateral trade restrictions or from undergoing drastic political upheavals through economic disruption), at least in a virtual stoppage of attempts at common policies.'

One does not have to share Stanley Hoffman's conclusions to agree that there is a serious political problem.

The significance of divergence in economic performance or developments is that, given a long enough period, it results in or is synonymous with the divergence of economic power. The level of GDP, the strength of a currency, the prestige of one's economic policies, the acceptance of the German model, all point to the core of the concept of relative national power.

Divergence of perceived national interests

Apart from the divergence of power, what matters at the political level in the Community is the divergence of perceived interests. Depending on the circumstances, these may cause conflicts, paralysis, or crisis in the Community.

The divergence of economic developments is neither a necessary nor a sufficient condition for political difficulties in the Community. It is not a necessary condition in that political problems can arise independently of or without the intervention of any divergence in economic developments, as the case of the Common Fisheries Policy shows. The dispute in this case is about who can catch what in waters that are regarded by some as Community waters and by others as national exclusive economic zones, and has little to do with (through it may have been exacerbated by) divergent GDP levels, price levels, or exchange rates. The divergence of economic developments is not a sufficient condition for the emergence of political difficulties, in that it need not always lead to such problems and in that, where it does result in political conflicts, these arise through the intervention of perceived national interests.

However, divergences of economic developments are significant because they increase the probability of a divergence of perceived interests. It is extremely difficult to establish any general laws about the evolution of perceived interests, which depend on a host of factors, including circumstances and situations, needs, trade-offs, ability to pay, relative strength or weakness, pressures, attitudes, etc. Nevertheless, divergences of economic developments, situations or performances may alter circumstances, upsetting delicately established compromises and affecting perceptions, changing abilities to pay, exacerbating pressures, and so on; and although one cannot be too precise ahead of events, it stands to reason that such changes are conducive to divergences of perceived interests. This may be particularly so in cases where common policies are based on the principle of uniformity, as with the CAP (Chapter 5) or the CCP (Chapter 6). The CAP was originally built on the idea of uniform prices, while the CCP was built on the concept of a uniform degree of protection *vis-à-vis* the outside world. These principles could not accommodate the divergent needs which were created by divergence economic developments.

Convergence of perceived national interests

Convergence of perceived national interests are the most important condition for progress in European integration or co-operation. However, what matters is not interests decreed immutably and unambiguously by God, nature or history, but interests as perceived by governments and ruling élites, and herein lies the hope for international co-operation, for interests can be defined in a narrow or wider sense, in a long-term or short-run perspective. Moreover, common interests are not only those which are naturally so, but those which are made to be so, through a long process of give and take and of learning to work together. Common interests, in other words, can be created. Sometimes in history, however, it may require the genius and vision of a Jean Monnet or Robert Schuman to make apparent and to create such a convergence of interests.

Despite the frequent divergences and occasional conflicts of interests, the member states share many common interests, some actually common, others potentially common. Moreover, decades of European integration have produced transnational European interests groups. These groups are to be found among trade unions, employers, farmers, environmental or ecological lobbies, regional movements, cultural groups, multinational companies, and at the level of specific industries (automobiles, chemicals, oil, steel, etc). There is also a transnational European awareness and perception of problems and values.

Policies

The main focus of political power and popular loyalty in the present age remains, however, the nation state. Integrated, supranationally managed and financed common policies on the lines of the CAP are not likely to be introduced in the foreseeable future, largely because of the negative lessons drawn from the experience of the CAP. The progress of European integration will probably therefore be via the co-ordination and convergence of national policies. It may be speculated that progress will be most notable in those areas in which convergences of perceived interests are more likely to take place or to be engineered. Such convergences are often easier to achieve in relation to the outside world than in relation to the distribution of costs and burdens in internal EEC matters. Foreign-policy co-operation may well offer many further possibilities in the future. It is also easier to achieve convergence when everyone stands to gain than when burdens and sacrifices have to be distributed. Thus, the newer and more rapidly expanding industries, the industries of the future as they are called, offer more scope for co-operation than do the problems of dealing with the declining industries.

Institutions

The need to reconcile divergences of perceived national interests among EC member states and to create convergences of such interests may lead to changes in the institutional and organizational set-up of the Community. At present, decision-making in the EC may, with some exceptions, be said to be characterized by three features: participation by all member states (in decision-making and perhaps to a lesser extent, in the implementation of common policies); decision by unanimity in the Council; and uniformity (in the implementation of common policies). Each of these principles makes agreement more difficult than otherwise would be the case.

We saw in Chapters 5, 6 and 7 examples of the *differentiated* application of a common policy: MCAs permit different prices for agricultural products, 'regional ceilings' enable each country to limit its imports of textile products, and the Community system of state aids for coal allows member states considerable freedom in granting such aids. Although procedures, formalities, and the discipline of other Community measures can go a long way in maintaining the appearance of a common policy, there must be a point at which increasing differentiation will simply lead to the collapse of the so-called common policy. Increases in the number of derogations from common rules and policies may also be thought to vitiate, eventually, the aim of integration.

Majority voting has sometimes been advocated as a way out of the institutional impasse affecting the EC. It is difficult, however, to visualize a member state being outvoted on an issue of great importance to itself and being forced to adopted measures against its will. This is not to say that the principle of unanimity could not be abandoned for minor questions.

It is useful, in my view to distinguish here between the rule of *unanimity* and the *veto*. The rule of unanimity says, 'Without my consent your decision does not bind me', and is a logical corollary of the principle of sovereignty. The veto declares, 'Without my consent there is no decision at all', and amounts to a power of blackmail not strictly required by the principle of sovereignty. The principle of unanimity combined with participation by all member states has given a power of veto to member states which may not be directly concerned or really interested in or capable of joining a proposed scheme. This has led to the floating of two formulas for accelerating progress in European integration or co-operation: *l'Europe à plusieurs vitesses*; and *l'Europe à géometrie variable*.

L'Europe à plusieurs vitesses

Known in English as a two-tier Europe (which has a slightly different connotation), this formula was attributed to the former West German Chancellor, Herr Willy Brandt, and was stated in the Tindemans Report on European Union[7] as follows:

> 'It is impossible at the present time to submit a credible programme of action if it is deemed abslutely necessary that in every case all stages should be reached by all the States at the same time. ... It must be possible to allow that:
> – within the Community framework of an overall concept of European Union as defined in this report and accepted by the Nine
> – and on the basis of an action programme drawn up in a field decided upon by the common institutions, whose principles are accepted by all,
>   (1) those States which are able to progress have a duty to forge ahead,
>   (2) those States which have reasons for not progressing, which the Council, on a proposal from the Commission, acknowledges as valid, do not do so,
>   – but will at the same time receive from the other States any aid and assistance that can be given them to catch the others up,
>   – and will take part, within the joint institutions, in assessing the results obtained in the field in question.
> 'This does not mean Europe *à la carte*; each country will be bound by the agreement of all as to the final objective to be achieved in common; it is only the timescales for achievement which vary.'

In theory, this formula has serious disadvantages: derogations may snowball, different classes or groups of members may emerge, and the unity and cohesion of the Community may be weakened. On the other hand, it may be the only way to go ahead with certain 'common policies' within the Community framework.

It should be noted that *l'Europe à plusieurs vitesses* is already a reality in some areas. The currency snake was an example, grouping the strong economies around the Federal Republic of Germany. The EMS is another illustration, with Italy being allowed a wider margin of fluctuation for its currency (6 per cent) than the others (2¼ per cent), and with the United Kingdom not participating in the exchange-rate and intervention mechanisms at all (but participating in the pooling of reserves).

L'Europe à géométrie variable[8]

This formula refers to the realization of common projects (such as the European Airbus) by a restricted number of member states; in other words, not all member states would participate and hence have a right of veto. Participation would be limited to those who are interested in joining and who are capable of making a useful contribution. The number of participants, however, may vary from project to project, hence the description 'variable-geometry'. The small number of participants has the advantage of making agreement easier and quicker and of facilitating efficient management.

The multi-speed and variable-geometry formulas share one characteristic: at any one point in time, not all member states will be participating in the programme or project. Only those which are interested in and capable of joining would do so. The variable-geometry formula may, however, go further in restricting voting power to those which are or will be participants, and hence in removing the possibility of veto by non-participants. It represents, therefore, a greater departure from the traditional mode of decision-making in the Community. The smaller and less-prosperous member states may see in this formula the germ of a directorate centred mainly on the Franco-German alliance.

Whatever the formula, it is certainly true that a convergence of interests will be easier to achieve with a smaller number of participants than with a large number. Relaxing the principle of uniformity may also help to reconcile divergent interests. Where either approach or both would lead European integration is not clear, and political science has yet to address itself to the question. The fear is that they may fail to create and to sustain a perceptional of a common political base for Europe.

1 For an analysis of how US automotive and computer companies organized their production on a Europe-wide basis, see Y.s. Hu, *The Impact of US Investment in Europe, a Case Study of the Automotive and Computer Industries*, New York, Praeger, 1973.
2 In March 1970 the Commission presented a *Memorandum on Industrial Policy in the Community*, and in may 1973 it submitted to the Council an *Action Programme in the Field of Technological and Industrial Policy*.
3 Imre Vajda, 'Integration and the national state', in: Imre Vajda and M. Simai (ed.), *Foreign Trade in a Planned Economy*, Cambridge, Cambridge University Press, 1971.

4 'A regulation shall have general application. It shall be binding in its entirety and directly applicable in all member states. A directive shall be binding, as to the result to be achieved, but shall leave to the national authorities the choice of form and methods. A decision shall be binding in its entirety upon those to whom it is addressed.' (Article 189 of the EEC Treaty)

5 The figures for the total amount of ECUs created, and the share of each member state, are not available (so far) from any statistical source. However, when the EMS was launched, the Commission reported that an intial supply of 23,000 million ECUs was created. The Bundesbank's *Monthly Reports* indicated a German ownership of 9,620 million ECUs in April 1979, and the Banque de France indicated an ownership of 4,588 million ECUs for the same month.

6 Stanley Hoffman, 'Domestic policies and interdependence', in: *OECD, From Marshall Plan to Global Interdependence*, Paris, 1978.

7 Leo Tindemans, *Report on European Union*, Brussels, 1976.

8 See Commissariat Général du Plan, *L'Europe: les vingt prochaines années*, Paris, La Documentation Française, 1980.

About the Author

Dr Hu was born in Tashkent in the USSR but grew up in Paris and Hong Kong. He studied Philosophy, Politics and Economics (PPE) at Oxford, where he also completed a D.Phil. in economics. He has worked as research fellow at Political and Economic Planning, London; as industrial economist at the World Bank, Washington DC; and as senior research fellow at Chatham House, London. He is now senior lecturer at the Administrative Staff College, Henley-on-Thames. He is the author of *The Impact of US Investment in Europe, a Case Study of the Automotive and Computer Industries*, New York, Praeger, 1973, and of *National Attitudes and the Financing of Industry*, London, PEP, 1976, and co-author of *Reshaping Britain*, London, PEP, 1974 and *Industry and Europe*, London, PEP, 1971. He has also written a number of articles and reports on other subjects.

Index